TOWARDS 'LEADERFUL' COMMUNITIES IN THE NORTH OF ENGLAND

Stories from the Northern Leadership Academy

Richard Thorpe, Jeff Gold, Lisa Anderson,
John Burgoyne, David Wilkinson & Becky Malby

Published by
Oak Tree Press
19 Rutland Street, Cork, Ireland
www.oaktreepress.com

© 2008 Northern Leadership Academy.

A catalogue record of this book is
available from the British Library.

ISBN 978-1-904887-21-8

Printed in Ireland by ColourBooks.

CONTENTS

Part 3: Taking Leadership Development Forward

FIGURES

THE NORTHERN LEADERSHIP ACADEMY

The Northern Leadership Academy (NLA) was created in 2006 as part of *The Northern Way* strategy to bridge the £30bn output gap between the North and the average for England. The NLA, a flagship initiative, has been given the task of supporting and stimulating leadership throughout the North, in order to generate measurable and sustainable growth.

The NLA is the result of a powerful collaboration between Lancaster University Management School, Leeds University Business School and the University of Liverpool Management School, supported by The Northern Way and the three Regional Development Agencies – NWDA, One NorthEast and Yorkshire Forward.

Together, the partners represent the very best modern thinking and expertise on leadership. Central to reducing the output gap is the elevation of leadership development and skill levels. By educating leaders to operate more successfully within their own environments, it is hoped that a new culture of dynamism and enterprise will cascade down through the workforce. This will result in the creation of 'leaderful' organisations that will be well-positioned to make the most of every economic opportunity in the years ahead.

The NLA is already delivering:

- A market-leading web portal that provides access to high-quality resources to help improve leadership skills. The portal provides connectivity across the region and disseminates good practice through sector-specific content.

- A programme of projects and pilots, carefully tailored to cluster needs.

- Dialogue with business representatives, based on field research and think-tank discussion and debate on what really works.

- A fellowship programme for PhD students researching into leadership at universities across the North.[1]

- The provision of regional centres and strategic spaces where leadership development can take place.

- An ongoing evaluation of programmes and methodologies, with a view to informing policy-makers on best practice.

---

[1] Clarkson, G.P (2008). *Developing Leadership Research: Papers from the Northern Leadership Academy Fellows Conference 2007*, Leeds: Leeds University Press.

AUTHORS

RICHARD THORPE is Professor of Management Development at Leeds University Business School, and Deputy Director of the Keyworth Institute. He has research interests in the areas of both leadership and entrepreneurship, and has been the academic lead for the Northern Leadership Academy's think-tank.

JEFF GOLD is senior lecturer in Human Resource Management at Leeds Metropolitan University. He is also an Enterprise Fellow at Leeds University Business School, working on developing a distributed network of centres and supporting engagement within the Yorkshire and Humberside Region.

LISA ANDERSON is a lecturer in Human Resource Management at the Liverpool School of Management. Her interests lie in the field of evaluation-led leadership development and her doctoral research focussed on the promotion of reflective learning in practitioners. Her role in the NLA think-tank was to oversee the evaluation of leadership development activities.

JOHN BURGOYNE is Professor of Management Learning at both Lancaster University Management School and Henley Management Centre. John's interests lie in the area of leadership and learning, and he has been a champion of management learning over the past 30 years.

DAVID WILKINSON is a freelance academic, working in the fields of management development, leadership and learning. David holds contracts at Leeds University Business School and has been instrumental in stitching the various threads of this book together.

BECKY MALBY is Director of the Centre for Innovation in Health Management at the University of Leeds. Her work focuses on the public and voluntary sectors and, as such, she has led the NLA's approach to our public and voluntary sector interventions.

ACKNOWLEDGEMENTS

This book has been 'assembled' from the activities of the think-tank in a very short period of time. Making it possible has been with the support of a good many people but, foremost, Barbara Butler and Rob Whieldon at Leeds and Anna Cockman at Lancaster. Jean Broad had a crucial role in pulling all the material together.

Cases for the text have been provided from two academic colleagues, both of whom undertook their doctorates in the area of leadership: George Boak and Susan Kirkcaldy. Richard Greenwood from Yorkshire Forward has supported our work most constructively and thanks are due to him and those colleagues throughout the region who have worked, and continue to work, with us to connect training and development to the managers and leaders who wish to develop themselves and their businesses.

Those colleagues, who together make the ideas of 'distributed leadership' come to life in this project, are already making a difference – they are: Ossie Jones, Alan McPherson, Owen Whitehouse, Luke Pittaway, Tim Clarke, Jane Davies, Steve Gibbs, Peter Wraith, Kevin Boles, Karen Cargill and David Rannaghan. Thanks are due to them all.

Richard Thorpe
March 2008

FOREWORD

Many, and I include myself one, considered that a book written by academics could never be properly accessible to policy-makers and practitioners. I am pleased to say that I have been proved wrong.

This is an important document. It is not yet the finished article, but rather a vital staging post on a journey that, hopefully, will unleash the potential of business in the north of England. It represents two years of leading-edge thinking by members of the three collaborating institutions: Lancaster, Leeds and Liverpool. It has been supported by a host of hard working non-academics, all trying to find a Holy Grail, capable of restoring productivity and competitiveness to the region.

The Northern Leadership Academy was created in 2006 with a virtually impossible brief: how to identify and implement a new leadership paradigm, capable of transforming businesses of all shapes and sizes in our area. It has been an intriguing journey, watching and occasionally helping these energetic and enthusiastic devotees explore the complex world of organisational leadership. The logistical and relationship challenge posed by the project was itself unbelievably taxing. How do you harness these disparate experts across a range of high-powered organisations, all working for differing ends and differing emphases? The answer turned out to be: *with great difficulty!*

However, despite the complexity, the short life of the NLA project has demonstrated clearly the power of combining the intellectual powers of the university sector in pursuit of a regional, if not a national, objective. The majority of the outcomes reported in this book have been from those working with the project's 'think-tank' and evaluation groups, but others also have made important contributions under Andrew Brocklehurst's leadership, notably Steve Kempster and his team at Lancaster and Fred Mahoney and his team at Liverpool.

This book represents the key learning points to date and, in some ways, is an end-of-project account of the ideas developed and contributions made. The aggregation of the intellectual contributions emerges from the range of activities undertaken, some conventional, some exploratory. Read it, mindful of the fact that, in terms of implementation, the project is really only in its early stages. Over the years, I have been a passionate advocate of radical employee engagement, but often I have been disappointed to see promising installations fail, due to the indifference or incapability of an organisational figurehead. The work on distributed leadership, espoused by the NLA academics, could provide an important contribution to the way we think about leadership and, in so doing, save so much initiative failure.

I commend the book to you, both as a source of learning and also as a testament to the legion of enthusiasts who, over the past two and a bit years, have made the NLA so exciting.

John J Oliver OBE
Chair, Northern Leadership Academy

PART 1:
CONTEXT & HISTORY

1

WHY LEADERSHIP,
WHY NOW, WHY THE NORTH?

T his chapter sets the scene by introducing the
background context in which the Northern
Leadership Academy (NLA) emerged.

It begins with the current issues and pressures that
engulf businesses, both in the UK and globally.
Thereafter, it continues with a description of the
context, especially as it relates to the much-cited
'North-South divide', namely the gap in prosperity
and economic performance between the UK's northern
and southern regions.

Existing policies and initiatives, their nature, and
characteristics then are accounted for, in the process
noting their virtues and shortcomings. Painting the
prevailing circumstances that influence organisations
in the North and the programmes that have been
instituted paves the way for the final part, which
formulates the rationale for the NLA.

THE STATE OF THE WORLD –
SOME BACKGROUND CONTEXT

The pace of change in the world economy is becoming faster by the day. There are noticeable shifts in the way business is conducted globally, including significant reductions in trade barriers between regions and countries, as well as ever-stiffening competition. These trends in part have been prompted, or expedited, by an increasing use of technology. Such fast-paced changes have had the effect of putting pressure on private and public organisations, the result being that knowledge and skills are now considered differentiating elements in an organisation's success. That is why successive UK governments have attempted to nurture a culture of entrepreneurship and continuous skills development. These are generic efforts to enhance the country's capabilities that all need acknowledgement. However, despite a plethora of initiatives that incorporate business advice services, such as Business Link and 'up-skilling' efforts by the Learning & Skills Council (LSC), among others, there are still deeper disparities that persist between the North and South of the UK. The phrase 'North-South divide' is often applied to refer to the varying level of prosperity and productivity between the northern and southern parts. But the North has not always lagged behind in innovation and productivity, for its history bears testament to the presence of successful industries and periods when the flow of people was in the opposite direction – from the South to the North. So, what might have happened that has led to the present scenario in the North?

Geographically, the 'South' consists of London, the South-West, the South-East, the East, and the East Midlands, while the 'North' comprises the other parts of England, Scotland and Wales. The gap between the two regions is explained by a number of factors. First, the advent of the Industrial Revolution and the subsequent creation of large industries meant a boom for northern cities. Businesses flourished, jobs were created and, as a consequence, a positive net migration to those areas occurred. This translated into high economic performance, exemplified by high rates of employment. But, with the decline of the mining and manufacturing sectors that formed the backbone of their business activities, the northern cities have witnessed a plunge in their economic performance over the last one or two centuries, in comparison to the South. Second, apart from the rate of employment, the north-south gap manifests itself in the level of skills. For instance, knowledge-based and highly-paid professions, including insurance, banking and other professional service firms, dominate the south. By contrast, the bulk of the low-wage, low-skill professions are found in the north, which further entrenches regional economic disparities and deepens levels of deprivation in the poorer areas. In essence, this is a question of productivity, understood as the aggregate wealth contributed by each worker. As a result, highly-paid professions generate more value to the locations where they operate. A third aspect, linked to productivity, that has blighted the North is a lower level of entrepreneurial activity when compared with the south. In general terms, the number of small firms created, and their growth, indicate the level of entrepreneurial activity of a region or country. Factors such as education and skills play a crucial role in the population's entrepreneurial awareness and the ability to run businesses successfully. Despite the occasional debate to the contrary, the achievement of qualifications still remains the main way in which the level of skills may be evaluated. In that respect, the south has fared better than the north. There are likely to be fewer people with qualifications in the north when compared to the south.

EXISTING POLICIES & INITIATIVES

There are numerous imperatives and initiatives that either are being undertaken or are ideal to be considered in order for the North to deal with the situation described above. First, it is important that the North strives to enhance its human capital (skills and knowledge), for it is this that leads to income generation, something the South has exploited. If that is achieved, the outcome is a cycle where prosperous and economically-thriving areas, with high incomes, attract highly-skilled people, perpetuating the already existing disparities. Focus on education is fundamental in trying to tackle the issue of human capital, since failure to raise the skill levels is bound to have an adverse effect. Much public money has been spent on various Government-backed vocational programmes to boost skills levels among the young. If good skills lead to a virtuous cycle of better productivity, high income and more highly-qualified people to an area, low education tends to have an opposite effect. For instance, if the businesses in a particular region are less competitive (or less productive), they are likely to demand lower skills, which means people lose the incentive to pursue better qualifications or skills. Previous research has described similar dynamics.[2] Finegold & Soskice (1988), for example, first formulated what they called 'low skills equilibrium', according to which an economy becomes stuck in a continuous and mutually-reinforcing spiral characterised by low skills and low wages. Secondly, a wider enterprising awareness needs to be created, which demands a concerted effort encompassing all levels of the educational and training systems, that is, schools, colleges and universities, but also among SMEs. Again, such strategic vision of nurturing a business mind-set among learners and smaller firms demands leadership to steer it. Incidentally, leadership and management have emerged as some of the focal points of the Northwest Regional Development Agency's *Regional Economic Review* (2002). After all, SMEs are often formed and run by owner-managers around whom the whole firm revolves. Thirdly, one of the *Lambert Review*'s (2003) recommendations was the promotion of innovation through a close collaboration between industry and university.[3] The Regional Development Agencies (RDAs) were suggested as key co-ordinators in such joint efforts between institutions of higher learning and companies. Together, the RDAs and the Department for Business, Enterprise & Regulatory Reform[4] manage the money allocated for regional schemes – for instance, they co-fund regional initiatives, one of which is the Regional Selective Assistance (RSA) scheme, introduced in the 1970s to alleviate deprivation and to create employment opportunities in poorer parts of England. The RSA's remit is to assist investments that are likely to create jobs. Similar organisations and development agencies undertake corresponding work in Scotland and Wales. All

---

[2]   Finegold, D. & Soskice, D. (1988). 'The failure of training in Britain: analysis and prescription', *Oxford Review of Economic Policy* 4(3): 21-53.

[3]   Lambert, R. (2003). *Lambert Review of Business-University Collaboration: Final Report*, London: HM Treasury.

[4]   Formerly, the Department for Trade & Industry (DTI).

these are attempts at ensuring that projects with prospects of having an economic impact in disadvantaged areas are promoted.

THE NEED FOR THE
NORTHERN LEADERSHIP ACADEMY

So far, we have described the nature of the North-South divide and also highlighted existing policy-driven initiatives and schemes to overcome the gaps in economic performance between the two regions. We also briefly indicated how leadership would have provided an inspiration under different scenarios. In this section, we present the case for the Northern Leadership Academy (NLA). Why the NLA?

The first point worth noting is that there is a need for more engagement between universities and industry. It must be said that there are existing relationships between firms and universities on research, but these are often limited or sporadic. A leadership academy like the NLA facilitates the creation of a forum where academics and practitioners can interact and collaborate. In turn, this makes it possible to establish connections between the regional strategies and visions designed to bridge productivity gaps, skills requirements and research outputs from the universities. Enhanced skills are central for the productivity development of the North. This is noted, for example, by DfES papers (2003; 2005).[5] A leadership academy that pulls together a diverse range of professionals makes it possible to cater to the immediate regional and sub-regional agendas, as well as to the longer-term prospects of the areas. Rather than just tackling the immediate challenges, it makes more sense to invest in long-term leadership and co-ordination. Indeed, the NWDA's *Regional Economic Review* stressed the value of developing enterprising skills, as well as leadership and management.

Another issue is that the work and approaches of the development agencies actively working in the North vary considerably. There are those that adopt a single approach to deal with virtually all enterprises and industries. Others place emphasis on working with certain sectors

---

[5]   DfES (2003). *21st Century Skills: Realising Our Potential*, Norwich: HMSO; DfES (2005). *Skills: Getting on in Business*, Norwich: HMSO.

– for example with knowledge-intensive organisations and clusters. Despite their acknowledged significance for raising the productivity and the general economic performance of the North, there is widespread confusion and duplication of activities among existing initiatives. The work and remit of organisations such as Business Link, Yorkshire Forward, training and business advisory providers, RDAs, and the NWDA often overlap. Further, these bodies tend to apply varied evaluation approaches, the bulk of which pay attention to policy-driven targets and provisions rather than to demand. As a consequence, SMEs may be confronted with uncertainties as to where to turn for advice and help. Therefore, co-ordination and synergy among the plethora of initiatives connected to the leadership theme appears to be a logical priority. The NLA contributes to the alignment and coherence of the diverse activities and provisions, in the process facilitating the optimisation of resource use. All these require strategic leadership in order to harness and link the various elements together. With its research expertise, the NLA network acts as a bridge that binds together the diverse parts under these circumstances.

The way leadership is understood forms a third theme that chimes well with the need for the NLA. As was discussed earlier, the North-South divide is exemplified by productivity gaps and precipitated by other societal dynamics. Prominent among these societal dynamics is the rate of innovation, which hinges to a great extent on investment decisions and overall leadership. However, as it was understood about 20 years ago, leadership was about the lone hero, who single-handedly inspired the whole organisation and created something from scratch. According to that way of thinking, the heroic leader was considered self-sufficient, aloof, and had limited contact with other people. The heroic leader directs others who wait for his instructions, visions, and insights. Of course, concentrating influence and responsibility on a particular individual has its downside. The idea that organisational members would wait to be instructed by their leader on what to do, instead of taking initiatives and creativity today is seen as being counter-productive to the success of any enterprise. For one, it risks instilling a culture of evading responsibility for one's actions. The concept of the heroic leader is also questioned for other reasons as well, since in the 1980s when the idea was popular, there was a widespread assumption that such leaders would operate under stable and predictable business environments. The environment is now increasingly volatile and uncertain, partly due to the forces of globalisation. The new way of thinking about leadership is one where diverse sections of the company have contributions to make, without negating the central role of the board or strategic directors as a collective entity. The new emphasis is on distributed leadership, where anybody in an organisation has the potential to make a contribution to the way the firm is run or led. Whatever their role or responsibilities, employees can participate in organisational problem-solving, work autonomously without close supervision, create new ideas and solutions to improve their work, and support the top management, including SME owner-managers. In sum, the prevailing perception of leadership is inclusive and does not limit itself to a select few whose heroic actions and successes are rehearsed at every turn. Instead, it embraces new ways of working, typified by networked organisational forms where knowledge and skills are distributed across individuals, divisions, firms and regions, and where leadership can emerge from any part of the interconnected system. When viewed in this way, leadership becomes 'distributed' rather than being concentrated in one place or person. In other words, it is a leadership that centres on entrepreneurial and communal orientation, and is not reliant on a small number of individuals. With the active participation of several Northern universities and the formation of working groups, including a strategic think-tank, the NLA is central to the development of a movement to promote networked and distributed leadership.

An imperative to create an environment conducive to creating a climate of enterprise is a final factor that offers a basis for the establishment of the NLA. The underlying rationale is that enhanced capabilities of the workforce offer a way out of the kind of downward spiral of deprivation and unskilled employment that affects the North. For their part, higher skills and knowledge have influence on where the knowledge-based firms that provide high-value products and services are located. This necessitates the combined effort of universities, from which the NLA membership mainly draws, and industry. While the participating universities' research outputs and consultancy are instrumental in introducing newer ideas and tools, industry members lead in the creation of favourable conditions by way of business parks, shared offices, and business incubators.

2

THE WORLD IN WHICH WE LIVE: REVIVING THE NORTH OF ENGLAND

T his chapter outlines the North's leadership successes, illustrating some of the areas where the North has led the world.

However, it reminds us that the managerial and entrepreneurial leadership of the past may not be the kind that will serve us well in the future.

Therefore, some of the changes and challenges that face us in the future are set out for consideration.

INTRODUCTION

The north of England, arguably, has played a major part in social, economic and cultural development on a global scale, over a long timescale but perhaps most obviously through being at the forefront of the Industrial Revolution, mainly through the textile industry in its various forms, and the associated patterns of global trade.

The very idea of management has been argued to be a consequence of the Industrial Revolution, and its first use in its modern form occurred when the mill owners of the north of England decided to hand over the running of their mills to someone else while they went to start another one or build a country home and take up the hunting, shooting and fishing lifestyle of the aristocracy. The 'managing agent' was the name given to the person running the mill on behalf of the owner – the first managerial role.[6]

The likely importance of management to economic and social development in the north of England is captured by the following quote:

> *'A country can have endless resources of all sorts but, unless management is applied to these factors, the productivity of the system will be close to zero. Moreover, the better the management, the greater the output will be. Management effectiveness is the critical factor in the economic system.'*[7]

Indeed, as the history of the north of England shows, once management is established, it does not just rely on locally-available resources – it has the capacity to import them, and similarly to serve global markets with the product.

The management capability in the north of England must have been considerable in this era. And later, with the establishment of the Manchester Business School in the 1960s, as one of the two American-import business schools (alongside London, and thus an early attempt at North-South balance), the north of England was the site of an

---

6   Child, J. (1969). *British Management Thought: A Critical Analysis*, London: Goe, Allen & Unwin.

7   Farmer, R.N. & Richman, B.M. (1964). 'A model for research in comparative management', *Californian Management Review* 7: 57.

attempt to import presumed-superior American management capability; earlier, the north of England cotton industry was held up in America as a model to follow.

HISTORICAL DEVELOPMENTS

In long-scale history, humanity has progressed through the stages of hunter-gathering (collecting animal and vegetable food where it is) to the agricultural era (growing crops and animals in controlled spaces), to the industrial era (from the farm to the factory, from land and the country to the town and the city), and now to the post-industrial era.

Each of these eras of growing and making things has been accompanied by parallel patterns of trading, moving from local to global. Globalisation is nothing new in these terms; world trade started in the agricultural era and accelerated in the industrial one.

In the North's industrial era, in its early stages, we must remind ourselves, the slave trade was a major part of the trade pattern associated with the cotton industry. The notorious 'trade triangle' took industrial products and trinkets to Africa to trade for slaves, the slaves to America and other destinations to exchange for cotton (a large proportion of the slaves ending up working on the cotton plantations), and the cotton back to the north of the UK for manufacture into cloth.

By today's standards, the slave trade is obviously morally reprehensible, though it must not have been, for the majority at the time, even though it was an era of stronger Christian belief. Indeed, the Protestant ethic, advocating hard work and thrift, delayed gratification and saving for the future, is argued to have created the conditions for the Industrial Revolution, through the mechanism of persuading people to put up with less than satisfying work and saving for the future rather than consuming now, thus creating the essential funds for investment and growth.

Although we have yet to discuss the post-industrial era, it is interesting to speculate on what the lessons from this are for today. As a foretaste, it will be argued that agriculture (culturing the land) was succeeded by manufacture (making with the hand) and then by mentofacture (making with the mind) and finally (for now?), spiroculture (finding a sense of meaningfulness in life).

Are there moral, ethical and social responsibility issues about current activities that will concern us in the future, as the slave trade does for the past? Possible issues that we can glimpse are to do with green issues and what happens at the very front-end of the more-globalised supply chains, where cheap labour may be exploited while, at the same time, extracting food and other commodities from previously local markets which kept the goods affordable to local people. Perhaps fair-trade campaigners are today's equivalent to yesteryear's anti-slavers.

Perhaps also, we can ask what trade patterns could do to sustain us in the contemporary era. Manufactured goods seem to be at least as much or more an import rather than an export, though there is still the possibility of the North taking or keeping a lead in high-added-value products on the basis of its historical 'first mover advantage'. Energy may have become a critical import, though there are possibilities reviving for nuclear and the possibility of re-expanding coal mining, if historical experience in this area can create a lead on coal-using technologies with acceptable green credentials.

Otherwise, exports have to be the product of knowledge work – design and financial services, consultancy and the like – and cultural products. The former are represented by financial and legal centres, like Leeds and Manchester; the latter by the major football clubs, like Manchester United, and cultural centres, like Salford, Liverpool, Sheffield and Gateshead, as well as the tourist industry.

Management and leadership development is also an evolved part of the post-industrial economy, the following quote from Hunter Davies showing where some of it fits into the ecology:

> *'But I've noticed a new development in the seventies. Many of those huge Windermere sort of houses, which the cotton magnates built during the Victorian era, are now being bought up by a completely new wave of self-made property tycoons, men with their own holding companies, who buy a castle in the Lakes for themselves and their families, though they officially call them management training centres. They move in computers and make it the centre of their operations, but it is also their home. These sort of people do have cultural leanings and are very keen to improve life generally in the Lake District.'*[8]

---

8   Davies, H. (1980). *A Walk around the Lakes*, Feltham: Hamlyn Publishing, p.217.

Education more generally now is a major post-industrial economic activity and one that is central to most of the main cities of the North, serving not only the UK but a global population, particularly in developing parts of the world, although things are moving in these markets, with countries becoming ever more self-sufficient, and so Northern universities are establishing campuses overseas as a response to the increasing state of maturity of the countries in which many find themselves.

Innovation also is of current and great concern. It is worth noting that new patterns of trade perhaps will create the conditions that stimulate the need to innovate. It has been said that the furniture firm Waring & Gillow began when Mr. Waring (or Gillow) found some teak logs lying on the quay at Lancaster port (for a brief period, Lancaster was a major North-West port, before the expansion of Liverpool). These logs had been used as ballast and had arrived at Lancaster when a cargo for one of the sides of the slave-trade triangle had not been available. As a consequence, he had had the idea of using the ballast to make furniture! In many ways, Waring & Gillow exemplified the post-industrial innovator and only remains in the North today as a brand and marketing operation, rather than as a manufacturer.

From this case, there are two questions we might pose: What are the new resources we can use that have been brought to the North, whether deliberately or by accident, and how might we be able to use these to establish and create new businesses?

New roles for old resources are relevant as well. An example here might be the re-development of the canal system, originally built for industrial transport and, briefly, a success performing this function, before being replaced by the rail network, and now revived as a leisure resource and heritage for the nation.

Whatever the changes, the eras we outline have grown successively shorter – from millions to thousands, to hundreds, to tens of years.

Although the hunter-gatherer era was never centred on the north of the UK, being mainly in the plains of the African continent, later eras have been more Northern-centric. Hawkshead, now in Cumbria, was where Wordsworth went to school, and other towns, just like Hawkshead, were major and prosperous centres of the wool trade (wool processing went on to be a major Northern industry in the next era).

In the hunter-gatherer era, Darwinian evolution, based on random variation between generations and natural selection by the survival of the fittest, was the basis of change over time.

Today, evolutionary psychologists[9] (Nicholson, 1997; Nicholson, 1998, 2005) argue that many of the personality characteristics that shape our behaviour today were shaped in that era, and are relatively 'hard-wired', that is to say innate and difficult to change. In terms of leadership, Nicholson argues that our emotional side, located in the older parts of our brain, is relatively stable, but the cognitive side, located in the newer, in evolutionary terms, cortex is amenable to change and learning. This bears on the old debate, relevant to our concerns today, as to whether leaders are born or made. The evolutionary psychology answer is that the will to lead is significantly innate, but the ability to do it well can be learnt. In practical terms, this translates into support for American Airlines' HR slogan:

'Recruit for attitude, train for skill'.

The industrial era was underpinned by humanity's increasing capacity to harness physical power – wind, water, coal, oil, gas, nuclear – and to convert these to electricity for easy distribution and use. The post-industrial era has been, and is being, triggered by humanity's increasing capacity to harness information – the IT revolution.

Although the development of computing has been a broad Anglo/American phenomenon, at least in its early stages, the north of the UK played a significant part, particularly when it came to the commercialisation of the outcome:

'The Manchester Machine: The earliest general-purpose stored-program electronic digital computer to work was built in Newman's Computing Machine Laboratory at Manchester University. The Manchester "Baby", as it became known, was constructed by the engineers F.C. Williams and Tom Kilburn, and performed its first

---

9	Nicholson, N. (1997). 'Evolutionary psychology: Towards a new view of human nature and organisational society', *Human Relations*, 50:1053-78; Nicholson, N. (1998). 'Seven deadly syndromes of management and organisation: The view from evolutionary psychology', *Managerial & Decision Economics* 19: 411-426; Nicholson, N. (2005). 'Objections to evolutionary psychology: Reflections, implications and the leadership exemplar', *Human Relations* 58(3): 393-409.

calculation on 21 June 1948. The tiny program, stored on the face of a cathode ray tube, was just 17 instructions long. A much-enlarged version of the machine, with a programming system designed by Turing, became the world's first commercially-available computer, the Ferranti Mark I. The first to be completed was installed at Manchester University in February 1951; in all, about 10 were sold, in Britain, Canada, Holland and Italy.

The fundamental logico-mathematical contributions by Turing and Newman to the triumph at Manchester have been neglected, and the 'Manchester machine' nowadays is remembered as the work of Williams and Kilburn. Indeed, Newman's role in the development of computers has never been sufficiently emphasised (due perhaps to his thoroughly self-effacing way of relating the relevant events).'[10]

The coming of the post-industrial era has meant the growth of knowledge work, which arguably has led to the new demand for leadership.

Factory workers need managing, but knowledge workers need leading. The difference can be explained in terms of Marxist theory: in the industrial model, the capitalist owns the means of production, the machine on the factory floor. The manager is hired to hire and organise the labour to operate it. Labour is dependent on access to the machine to earn its living. In the post-industrial era, the knowledge worker owns the means of production, his or her own brain. They can work as independent sole traders, consultants, or in small self-owned firms and partnerships, as they often do. To work for a larger organisation, they need leadership, transactional or transformational, to persuade them to work to the organisation's agenda.

The coming of the post-industrial era does not mean the end of agriculture and manufacture, but it does transform them.

With the coming of the industrial era, the farm became increasingly mechanised – the only difference between the farm and the factory is that, in the factory, the goods go through the machine but, on the farm, the machine goes over the goods – the tractor towing its array of implements over the crops. In the case of battery-farming of chickens, pigs, etc., we have the agricultural factory.

---

[10]   *Source:* http://plato.stanford.edu/entries/computing-history.

With the coming of the post-industrial era, we find increasingly the factory controlled by information technology – robots, computer-controlled production lines. The people move from the factory floor to the control room and the back offices designing the control systems. We have the 'lightless factory floor' – lighting is not needed, because there is nobody there.

This applies on the farm too – the tractor, perhaps, is spraying crops with a pesticide/fertiliser treatment, controlled by a satellite link to the fertiliser firm's computer, according to a season schedule devised by its knowledge workers.

The same applies to trading – major ships have shrinking crews and increasing navigational control from head office knowledge workers, and knowledge products travel the internet and intranets by fibre-optic cable, microwave transmission and satellite.

Organisations themselves become more virtual, in three ways:

- People spend more time at workstations, which can be anywhere – in India, or at home or on the move.

- More of the interaction within organisations is virtual – virtual meetings, virtual teams, virtual projects, working with shared databases and the like.

- Organisations increasingly relate to their customers and suppliers globally – as exemplified by Amazon bookshops.

It is interesting to note that the North of the UK, and in fact the UK in general, seems to have more of small businesses active in IT, but less of the large ones, like SAP in Germany – an opportunity there, perhaps.

The spiroculture era brings the development of brands that can be identified with by both consumers and employees – for example, branded sports shirts where a £50 T-shirt costs 50p to make in China or India, and 50p to transport and distribute; the remaining £49 pays for the brand, the image to identify with.

Service is valued and judged by the feel-good factor of customer care, as much as by the effectiveness of the service itself.

Shopping malls become the new cathedrals, where people do not just get the goods and services that they physically need, but search for that new 'thing' that will make their life more meaningful.

AND SO TO LEADERSHIP

Our understanding of the world is based on what has happened in the past, our actions are in the present and the consequences that we hope will follow from them are in the future.

The world is not a predictable machine, but a complex system with emerging properties that may, and almost certainly will, surprise us.

The historical analysis presented here makes some kind of sense, though it almost certainly misses things out. However, this is understanding in retrospect. For the people at the time, there were always surprises, as there are and will be for us today and in the future.

However, some patterns and practical truths run forward over time, for a period, if not forever. The world is not a random lottery that we wake up to afresh each day. Instead, we face the challenge for an initiative like the Northern Leadership Academy to secure the prosperity of a region in the future through leadership development initiatives in the present, based on lessons from the past, and supplemented by our judgement, imagination and intuition.

The situation is a bit like driving in the fog – we can see a little way clearly, some way vaguely, and beyond that not at all. New things emerge first as vague shapes, some of which become significant, others not. The road we travel may continue the general direction we have come from, but there may be surprising twists and turns.

In this metaphor, the lessons are clear: try to drive within our limits (safe stopping distance), use our best guesses and judgements as to what lies ahead, be alert for new events and as prepared as possible to identify and implement changes to meet them.

We cannot guess today what, if anything, will come beyond mentofacture and spiroculture. We have noted the shortening of the eras of these kinds, so something new may be with us soon or amongst us now. On the other hand, we know that forever exponentially-accelerating rates of change are not sustainable, so perhaps we are about to settle back to a more stable era. Who knows?

THE NORTH OF THE UNITED KINGDOM

Returning to the theme of the North, it is interesting to note that it, or at least most of its major cities, have undergone a post-industrial revival, albeit one that could go further.

Most of the cities have become vibrant residential areas, having been largely offices in their centres, surrounded by factories and residential areas. Areas like Trafford Park in Manchester visibly have moved on to a second generation of commercial activity.

Ports, like Liverpool, Newcastle / Gateshead and Salford Quays have revived as centres for culture and the media industries.

Leeds is regarded as the most significant legal centre outside London, but now with global aspirations and a 'powerhouse of legal talent' – according to the website of Leeds Legal.[11]

The macro leadership question is how to maintain and accelerate the long-term lead of the North in global development.

This will need attitude and skill. If attitude is somewhat innate, let us hope there is enough of it. Perhaps there is. An apocryphal Mancunian, on being told that Birmingham had claimed to be Britain's second city, said "That's funny, I thought it was London!".

---

[11]   http://www.leedslegal.co.uk/.

3

MODELS OF LEADERSHIP: WHY SOME ENDURE & OTHERS ARE INAPPROPRIATE

T his chapter begins by making sense of leadership, by first discussing the nature of the enduring realities of leadership when contrasted with management, before moving to highlight again the very real long-term changes in work, organisations and society of which our approach to leadership needs to be a part.

The chapter then reviews what are generally considered to be the main approaches to understanding leadership and concludes with a discussion on leadership development and the concept we return to at the end of the book – evaluation-led leadership.

LEADERSHIP

Despite the fact that Keith Grint[12] has argued that leadership is an 'essentially contested concept', and Stogdill[13] has pointed out that there are almost as many definitions of leadership as there are authors on the topic, four propositions seem relatively secure and useful:

- Leadership and management are about dealing with the boundary between order and chaos – management slightly more towards the order side, leadership to the chaos/complexity one. The trick is to balance maintaining the old (unless it is positively dysfunctional) with developing the new, while managing the replacement by the latter of the former.

- Leadership has become more important in the mentofacture / spiroculture eras, as management did in the era of manufacture.

- We should not forget good management is added to, not replaced by, leadership. Well-led change needs good management to implement and maintain it. A well-managed base camp to retreat to when leadership encounters with chaos and complexity get difficult is desirable, indeed necessary, for a chance to survive to fight another day.

- Leadership has become more distributed, it is partly by 'the few', who are still significant in their influence, but it is also by 'the many', who have increasing impact. Leadership is partly human capital, in individuals, but partly also social capital, in collectives: teams, whole organisations, perhaps sectors and regions. This makes it particularly challenging as a target for leadership development. However, 'blended' leadership is a useful idea: followers, individually and collectively, partly want the empowerment to make their own choices, but they often also want to have someone, or somewhere, to look to for a sense of direction.[14]

12   Grint, K. (2000). *The Arts of Leadership*: Oxford: Oxford University Press.

13   Stogdill, R.M. (1974). *Handbook of Leadership*, New York: The Free Press.

14   Collinson, D. (2005). 'Dialectics of leadership', *Human Relations* 58(11): 1419-42.

DEALING WITH THE BOUNDARY BETWEEN ORDER & CHAOS / COMPLEXITY

If an idea is repeated in different forms over a long period of time, this may well be because it represents an enduring truth.

Arguably, the following are saying more or less the same thing, about organisations dealing with the boundary between order and chaos/complexity, with management and leadership being specifically involved in doing this:

- Herb Simon[15] made the distinction between programmed and unprogrammed work in organisations, and argued that the former is concentrated in technical specialisms and functions, and that administration/management/leadership is left with the rest (the shift from talking about administration to management to leadership seems to be along the same continuum, but we note that the current debate between management and leadership is quite similar to the one between administration and management a few decades ago. Management used to be on the complexity side, now it has crossed to the order side).

- Burns & Stalker,[16] dealing with the topic of innovation which concerns us so much today, made the distinction between a mechanistic and organic way of understanding organisation and how it works. This is not a 'goodie'/'baddie' distinction, unless too much reliance is put on the mechanistic model, the rebellion about which was a great theme of the 1960s.

- Reg Revans,[17] the developer of action learning, made the distinction, in terms of what can be learnt by managers/leaders, between 'P' for 'programmed' and 'Q' for 'questioning' knowledge. Programmed knowledge is known solutions to known problems; questioning is the search for as yet unknown solutions to only fuzzily-sensed problems.

---

[15] Simon, H.A. (1957). *Administrative Behavior* (2nd ed.), New York: Macmillan.

[16] Burns, T. & Stalker, G.M. (1961). *The Management of Innovation*, London: Tavistock.

[17] Revans, R.W. (1998). *The ABC of Action Learning*, London: Lemos & Crane.

- Ralph Stacey[18] and others developed complexity theory, which explicitly sees organisations as open systems maintaining a balance between order and chaos/complexity.

- Finally, Warren Bennis[19] and others, addressing the management/leadership debate directly, cast leadership as the visionary, creative, inspirational, energising aspect of organising – in contrast with the routine and operational role of management.

THE NEW IMPORTANCE OF LEADERSHIP

The argument for the new importance of leadership in the post-industrial age has been rehearsed (see **Chapter 2**). It is that knowledge workers, being the owners of their own means of production (their brains), are much more autonomous than the traditional worker who is dependent on organisation and management for access to the machines through which they can earn a living.

This, and the dynamic speed with which knowledge-based organisations can change their business models, and the dynamic speed with which the networks within which they operate can change, means that leadership is about people and strategy, and management is about tasks and operations.

Perren & Burgoyne,[20] in a review of the management/leadership competency literature, produced the model shown in **Figure 3.1**, which shows how this distinction underlies most thinking and research on the topic.

Despite the shift of emphasis to leadership, the point has been made about the continuing importance of management. Organisations make their living, or justify themselves, by their managed existing goods and services, and it is these that are needed to invest in the lead innovation and change.

---

18   Stacey, R.D. (1992). *Managing Chaos: Dynamic Business Strategies in an Unpredictable World*, London: Kogan Page; Stacey, R.D. (2003). *Strategic Management & Organisation Dynamics: The Challenge of Complexity*, London: Prentice-Hall.

19   Bennis, W. & Nanus, B. (1985). *Leaders*, New York: Harper & Row.

20   Perren, L. & Burgoyne, J.G. (2002). *The Management & Leadership Nexus: Dynamic Sharing of Practice & Principle*, London: Council for Excellence in Management & Leadership, p.13

FIGURE 3.1: THE SKILLS & COMPETENCIES REQUIRED IN LEADERSHIP & MANAGEMENT

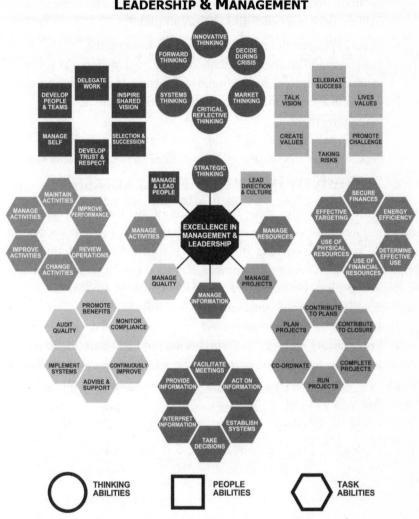

Explorations in the world of chaos and complexity are inherently risky and dangerous and an orderly base camp to retreat to between forays is essential.

A REVIEW OF LEADERSHIP MODELS

There have been a number of approaches to understanding leadership over the years, which may represent, in part at least, the change from leadership in the industrial to the post-industrial era. Very briefly, they have been:

- **Trait theory:** It depends on personality characteristics, which themselves may be 'born' or 'bred'.[21]

- **Functional:** It's a job; look after 'task, team and individual' – the classic model developed by John Adair[22] for military leadership training and still in use there.

- **Style:** Being at the right place on the authoritarian/democratic dimension: tell, sell, consult or join.

- **Balance:** Getting this right in terms of concern for people, concern for task.[23]

- **Situational:** Taking the style and balance dimensions as important, but arguing that there is no one right way, only what is appropriate to the situation.[24]

- **Power use:** Leadership as using power in its different forms: formal, expert, resource, charismatic, political and reputational.

- **Transactional vs. transformational leadership:** Negotiating effort for reward vs. creating new vision of fulfilment. Very much like the management/leadership debate.[25]

- **Dialogical:** Leadership as making sure that the right conversations take place to stimulate the dialogue that creates reality.[26]

---

[21]   See the revival of this debate in Nicholson, N. (2000). *Managing the Human Animal*, London: Texere Books.

[22]   Adair, J. (1983). *Effective Leadership*, London: Gower.

[23]   Blake, R.R. & Mouton, J.S. (1964). *The Managerial Grid*, Houston: Gulf Publishing.

[24]   Hersey, P. & Blanchard, K. (1988). *Management of Organisational Behavior*, Englewood Cliffs, NJ: Prentice-Hall.

[25]   Alimo-Metcalfe, B. & Alban-Metcalfe, J. (2005). 'Leadership: Time for a new direction?', *Leadership* 1(1): 51-71.

[26]   Drath, W. (2001). *The Deep Blue Sea: Rethinking the Source of Leadership*, San Francisco: Jossey-Bass.

Dialogical leadership, in particular, seems very much to be the form of leadership for the post-industrial era.

In particular, it offers a resolution to the problem not of *what* leadership is, but *where* it is. There has been much interest in recent years in distributed or shared leadership – the idea that leadership is not in one or a few individuals, but dispersed throughout an organisation.[27]

Figure 3.2 shows the options on two dimensions: leadership by the few *vs.* leadership by the many, and leadership as a property of individuals (human capital) *vs.* leadership as a property of the collective (social capital) – this distinction is due to Day.[28]

FIGURE 3.2: WHERE IS LEADERSHIP CAPABILITY?

Human & Social Capital

Leadership by the Few	HERO		TOP TEAM
Leadership by the Many	EMPLOYEE EMPLOWERMENT		CULTURE, STRUCTURE & TECHNOLOGY

Human Capital: individual capability	**Social Capital:** collective capability

DEVELOPMENT	EDUCATION, TRAINING & DEVELOPMENT	HYBRIDS	ORGANISATION CHANGE & DEVELOPMENT INITIATIVES

As a target for leadership development, the human capital/social capital distinction mirrors the distinction between, on the one hand, education, training and development, which targets human capital, and organisation development, which targets social capital.

Arguably, the majority of the effort is going into education, training and development, and perhaps we need to renew our efforts to make

---

27 Pedler, M. & Burgoyne, J.G. (2006). 'Distributed leadership', *View - NHSIII Journal* (11): 20-21.

28 Day, D.D. (2001). 'Leadership development: A review in context', *Leadership Quarterly* 11(4): 581-613.

organisation development work, and also the hybrids that combine the two.

The idea of dialogical leadership offers a way in which the individual can stimulate or facilitate the collective, distributed leadership of the many, thus combining these different forms.

Rather than a full-scale switch from individual, heroic leadership to a totally-distributed form, this would enable a form of 'blended' leadership, as suggested by Collinson & Collinson,[29] in which people have both substantial empowerment but also somewhere to turn for a sense of direction.

LEADERSHIP DEVELOPMENT

Leadership development, in the main, cannot be treated as straightforward human resource development/training – known processes for known outcomes, for known benefits. Having said that, there are some basic 'literacy' skills for management and leadership that can be learnt in this way and, if they are missing, this is the best and most cost-effective starting point.

The driving in the fog metaphor of leadership is probably the most useful – leadership development needs to be focused on this. This includes the specifics of particular journeys and the general skill of alertness, learning to learn. But being a good driver – see the point in the previous paragraph – is a necessary, not sufficient, condition.

The development process needs to mirror the leadership process – practice in working on the boundary between the personal known and unknown, safety and risk, with plenty of opportunity for experimentation and feedback in a situation where protection from the extreme consequences of risk is maintained.

Leadership development needs to be targeted on the few and the many, and on both human and social capital, and on a system based on blended leadership. This calls for education, training and development, and organisation development, and hybrid initiatives that combine the two.

---

[29] Collinson, M. & Collinson, D. (2005b). *'Blended Leadership': Employee Perspectives on Effective Leadership in the UK FE Sector*, Working paper series, London: DfES, Centre for Excellence in Leadership.

We must bear in mind the evolutionary psychology principle that the will to lead may be somewhat innate, but the ability to do it well is learnt. This means we can think about how to be selective about whom we invest leadership development effort in – to sow the seeds on fertile ground.

This reminds us that leadership development is part of a 'bundle', a strand in a rope if you like, where the strength of the rope is greater than the sum of the parts, and the realisation of this depending on the way in which the strands are woven together.

The three main parts of the bundle are acquisition, development and utilisation. Selecting people or teams to lead, or to be developed to lead, comes under the heading of acquisition. Development is what we have been talking about in the previous section. Utilisation is about making the best use of the leadership capability that we already have, or may develop. Arguably, before we embark on the relatively expensive and time consuming activity of leadership development, we should make sure that we are making the best use of the leadership capability that we already have and, when we do, we should be clear about how we expect the newly-developed capability that we hope to create will impact on the organisation. This should help us focus the process, outcome and effects of leadership development initiatives.

Acquisition covers the processes of internal and external organisational recruitment to leadership roles, but also the acquisition of teams and whole organisations with leadership capability, or the ability to add value because of the lack of it.

Development is what we are talking about here, and includes individual and organisational development, formal and informal learning, and is always a supplement to the 'natural' learning that is going on anyway.

Utilisation covers all the practices that determine whether leadership capability actually gets used, and normally includes performance management, career planning, reward systems and 'hard' organisation development – the re-structuring that creates new leadership roles.

Leadership development, for good reason, has been based largely on experiential learning approaches, such as Kolb's theory and well-known cycle.[30] The 'good reason' is that, in operating across the boundary from order into chaos/complexity, there are no rules to be followed – they have to be discovered and invented *in situ*.

However, much leadership development in the past has focused on experiential learning for the individual and, in recent years, this has been criticised[31] to the extent that it fails to take account of the learning that takes place in collective ways and through the influence of others. Experiential learning then needs to be supplemented by collective approaches, drawing on insights from more social theories of learning, like situated learning theory.[32]

EVALUATION OF LEADERSHIP DEVELOPMENT

The challenge for evaluation is to learn the lessons from what has worked well – and less well – in the past, and to apply these to what we do now for the future.

Given what we have said, leadership development evaluation is not just another occupational area to be tackled by generic principles of training evaluation.

It needs to recognise that leadership development works as much through 'generative' causation (creating the conditions where things can change and move on to destinations as yet unknown) as 'successionist' causation (achieving predictable and pre-known outcomes).

Given that the world does not seem to be a predictable machine, but an open system with emergent properties, there are two things that we can do.

First, we can identify things that will not work, and hence usefully narrow the range of choices for future action (you cannot make an omelette without breaking eggs, but breaking eggs does not guarantee that you get an omelette).

---

30   Kolb, D.A. (1984). *Experiential Learning*, Englewood Cliffs, NJ: Prentice-Hall.

31   Holman, D. Pavlieka, K. & Thorpe, R. (1996). 'Re-thinking Kolb's theory of experiential learning: The contribution of social construction and activity theory', *Management Learning* 25(4): 489-504.

32   Lave, J. & Wenger, E. (1991). *Situated Learning: Legitimate Peripheral Participation*, Cambridge: Cambridge University Press.

Secondly, we can identify 'mechanisms' that have worked in the past, and could, but cannot be guaranteed to, work in the future. For example, heightened self-awareness and understanding of one's impact on others – one popular avenue for leadership development – can lead to improved leadership behaviour, performance and outcomes, but is not guaranteed to do so. This depends on for whom, and in what circumstances. This does not suggest that some determinist contingency model will work either – this would just be a more complicated version of the machine.

'Circumstances' are always combining and recombining in new forms, events never repeat themselves exactly. However, we can identify mechanisms that can work and attempt to design situations where they have a greater likelihood of doing so.

4

A NEW WAY OF THINKING: UNDERSTANDING INFLUENCE & DISTRIBUTION

L eadership is a complex and ever-changing area of study. There are few areas of agreement and many theories and theorists.

This chapter seeks to unpack some of the key concepts, ideas and approaches to distributed leadership, and its application for business organisations.

Distributed leadership forms the foundation of the NLA's views on leadership and entrepreneurial development and has influenced directly the structures in place to cascade leadership activities and programmes more widely.

INTRODUCTION

The conventional paradigm of leadership describes the heroic leader as one who is either 'born, not made' or, alternatively, selected then developed. The outcome of this view of leadership is dependent upon its appropriateness. Leaders are seen as strong and insular, self-sufficient but often inaccessible (and consequently, often lonely). The dependency of followers often becomes a conditioned response: followers wait to be told what to do. Effort goes into finding the 'right' leader as the solution to the problems of the community.

This idea of leadership certainly has remained the dominant force in the North, and elsewhere, for many years. It chimes nicely with a view of organisations as 'machines', where leaders co-ordinate and command the various 'parts'. This view places some people at the helm and others, the followers, who respond, elsewhere … below. The factories of the North understood this well, and we know this is unlikely to change without a radical challenge. However, if the North is to break free of the restraint of the past, we felt that we needed new ideas about leadership.

Certainly, there are ideas that remain focused on individuals, but an emerging idea of distributed leadership seemed to provide something different. As we will explain below, it is an idea that seems more suited to where we want to go, offering an emphasis on collective endeavour, shifting influence, webs of interconnection, uncovering and removing the restraint from the past and, mostly, the prospect of setting organisations on a path of learning that embraces knowledge-based and high value-added economic and social development.

DEFINITIONS

There are few clear definitions of distributed leadership and it has been said that those that exist appear to differ from each other, sometimes considerably and sometimes more subtly.[33] A distributed leadership perspective on organisations considers the way the leadership function is shared or distributed amongst those with the ability and experience necessary to ensure the function is carried out to the benefit of the wider organisation. Jim Spillane,[34] a leading writer and practitioner in the field of distributed leadership, explains that distributed leadership is centrally concerned with leadership practice, framed in a particular way. In short, it is a product of the joint interactions of leaders, others and aspects of their situation (such as the tools they use and the routines or procedures they adopt). Such a distributed view of leadership shifts the focus from the typical or traditional leader (a chief executive or a school or college headteacher or principal), to an intricate and complex web of leaders, followers and their situation that gives rise to leadership practice – as expressed in **Figure 4.1**.

FIGURE 4.1: LEADERSHIP PRACTICE

Source: Spillane (2006).

---

[33]   Bennett, N., Wise, C., Woods, P. & Harvey, J.A. (2003). *Distributed Leadership: A Review of Literature*, Nottingham: National College for School Leadership.

[34]   . Spillane, J. (2006). *Distributed Leadership*, San Francisco: Wiley.

Therefore, as distributed leadership is focused upon leadership practice, it moves beyond the typical and traditional explorations and examinations of leadership, to a focus upon roles, responsibilities and functions and the related interactions that take place. To help us think more clearly about what this actually means, Spillane suggests that we consider the performance of a two-partnered dance. Whilst the actions of each partner are crucial, much (if not, all) of the performance of the dance takes place through the interactions of the dancing partners. The practice is between the two dancers, and an account of the actions of each partner alone would not capture the practice that took place. Each dancer influences, and responds to, the other. Despite notions of one person taking the lead, the dance itself requires a process of mutual influence and response; without this, there is no dance.

Recent work, carried out in the UK, examining programmes of study designed to develop leaders, similarly indicates that leadership action or practice is part of a chain of events – leading to multiple actions, drawing upon a variety of tools, which are focused upon a number of discrete objects. This is, in effect, a system of inter-related activities:

> "... the action of one person only makes sense as part of a pattern of relationships, which form the collective activity".[35]

Such distributed leadership organisations (where roles and responsibilities are shared) therefore are distinct from typical or traditional organisations (where roles and responsibilities reside in the sole leader). One suggestion is that sole or individualised approaches to leadership represent one end of a leadership continuum – the other being one where responsibilities are shared collectively or collaboratively between a number of different leaders.[36] This is summarised in **Figure 4.2**.

---

[35]   Ross, L., Rix, M. & Gold, J. (2005). 'Learning distributed leadership: Part 1', *Industrial & Commercial Training* 37(3): 130-137.

[36]   Rodgers, H., Frearson, M., Gold, J. & Holden, R. (2003). *International Comparator Contexts: The Leading Learning Project,* London: Learning & Skills Research Centre.

FIGURE 4.2: A CONTINUUM OF APPROACHES TO LEADERSHIP

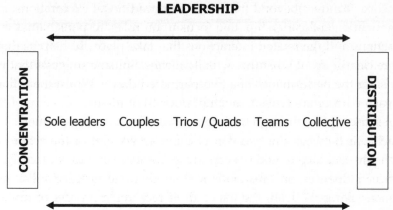

TYPES & FORMS

From a considerable review of education-related literature, it is suggested that there are three distinct elements of the concept of distributed leadership:

- Distributed leadership highlights leadership as an emergent property of a group or network of interacting individuals. Within a distributed approach, people work together in such a way that they pool their initiative or expertise. The resultant outcome is a product or energy, greater than the sum of their individual actions.

- Distributed leadership suggests openness of the boundaries of leadership; for example, others not typically involved in leadership roles and duties might have something useful to add to how an organisation is run and managed effectively.

- Distributed leadership entails the view that varieties of expertise are distributed across the many, not the few. Whilst some acts of leadership may be initiated by a small number of people, it is then for others to adopt, adapt and improve them for their own local circumstances.

These formulations of types of distributed leadership fit with Gronn's[37] analysis of the subject. His work indicates that, in relation to distributed leadership, no one person is an expert on everything within an organisation. Rather, the key activities within an organisation are performed by specialists, who rely on collaborative and reciprocal relationships. Therefore, this eliminates assumptions about leadership only ever residing in one individual.

Further and complementary understandings and definitions are put forward by Spillane and his colleagues,[38] who, in various pieces of research and exploratory work, have developed classifications for types of distribution (see below). Each of these types involve and require different relationships and attract different dependencies. These, in turn, bring forward similar and distinct challenges for leadership practice:

- **Collaborative distribution** characterises leadership practice that is stretched over the work of two or more leaders, who work together in place and time and execute the same leadership routine, such as facilitating a faculty meeting. The co-practice in this situation is similar to that in basketball, in which players must interact with one another, passing to team-mates when they stop dribbling and working to set one another up to shoot.

- **Collective distribution** characterises practice that is stretched over the work of two or more leaders who enact a leadership routine by working separately but interdependently. The interdependencies are akin to those in basketball or cricket, in which players at bat perform alone, but their actions, in interaction with that of the pitcher or bowler, collectively produce the practice.

- **Co-ordinated distribution** refers to leadership routines that involve activities that have to be performed in a particular sequence. The interdependency in this situation is similar to that in a relay race in track; the co-performance of the relay race depends on a particular ordered sequence.

---

[37]   Gronn, P. (2000). 'Distributed properties: A new architecture for leadership', *Educational Management & Administration* 28(3): 317-338.

[38]   Try the website at http://www.sesp.northwestern.edu/dls/; well worth visiting, with many papers, tools and ideas available for download.

Although the majority of the currently-available literature on distributed leadership focuses upon schools as organisational settings, such an approach can have useful application outside of school-based education. It can be considered and applied in other work settings where there is a focus on autonomous work and joint responsibility for that work (in terms of who does it and when it is done). Recent work indicates that more and more organisations will embrace notions of distributed leadership and use it as a model for organisational management and development. This will be particularly so for knowledge-based work and where workers are geographically dispersed. The effect will be to make traditional notions of the single organisational leader obsolete.

Can it work?

"If we are to start developing our collective leadership, then we also need to start ditching the recipe-approach to leadership: there are no 'seven-ways-to-guaranteed-success, because there are no guarantees, and there are no guarantees because no one individual can determine the outcome of collective efforts. Leadership is not like following a cooking recipe, because the ingredients that leaders use are not dead but live, not compliant but resistant."[39]

Critics of distributed leadership interpret the term as meaning the same as a number of other recent approaches to leadership. However, Spillane comments upon the differences that exist between this form of leadership and others such as collaborative leadership, co-leadership, and democratic leadership.

Although, by its very definition, collaborative leadership is distributed across two or more individuals, it does not necessarily follow that all distributed leadership is collaborative; it may be more or less so given the situation. This comment also holds when comparing distributed leadership to democratic leadership. Whilst distributed leadership enables and encourages leadership to be stretched over a number of leaders, this does not necessarily happen in a democratic or even-handed way. In some work situations, more or less leadership responsibility may be held by certain individuals.

---

[39] Keith Grint, *The Times*, 8 March 2005.

Co-leadership occurs when:

"... power and responsibility are dispersed [among] ... co-leaders with shared values and aspirations, all of whom work together towards common goals".[40]

However, Spillane's interpretation of distributed leadership indicates that there may be instances where leaders do not have exactly the same shared values and goals within the organisation.

There are also differences between distributed leadership and other progressive forms of leadership, such as transformational leadership. One key difference here is that the distributed approach focuses upon the practice of leadership, rather than on the empowering approach and actions of the hierarchical leader. As such, distributed leadership places leadership power with a range of individuals.

Distributed leadership does not negate the impact or requirement of leadership at the top, but requires this leadership as part of a wider leadership capability, where the social capital of the organisation is harnessed. Distributed leadership is leadership in practice 'stretched over the social and situational contexts' of the organisation. It is a model where the leadership effort is a product of the context, the people and leaders' thinking and behaviour. There is evidence that it is at work, whether leaders at the top can see it or not.

A year-long review of the evidence relating to schools, examined a single connection:[41] Does the work of a school leader (the headteacher) impact on student / pupil outcomes?

It was found that the impact of such leaders was mediated by others – in other words, leadership was distributed through staff, parents, the wider community and, in that distribution, it impacted on students' performance. It needs to be recognised by the leaders at the top that, by relinquishing power to others in the system and promoting interdependency, they become part of a process that creates powerful leadership.

---

[40] Heenan, D.A. & Bennis, W. (1999). *Co-leaders: The Power of Great Partnerships*, New York: Wiley, p.5.

[41] Bell, L., Bolam, R., & Cubillo, L. (2002). *A Systematic Review of the Impact of School Leadership & Management on Student / Pupil Outcomes*, Research Evidence in Education Library 1, London: EPPI-Centre, Social Science Research Unit, Institute of Education.

In essence, distributed leadership is different from traditional or typical forms of leadership; it requires organisations to think, act and behave in different ways. It relies upon a variety of factors to become effectively implemented. These include considerations in relation to:

- Control / autonomy within the organisation.
- The structure of the organisation.
- The social and cultural context within which the organisation, and the people within it, operate.
- The initiators of the change in concentration to a distributed approach.
- The 'position' and status of formal and informal leaders within an organisation.
- The dynamics of teams within an organisation (how they are formed and how they work).
- The extent to which distributed leadership has become institutionalised within the organisation.
- How conflicts are resolved in terms of accountabilities and goal-setting.[42]

The move towards interpreting leadership as something distributed represents a challenge for those individuals with leadership formally as one of their roles. It would be naive to play down the structural, cultural, legal and political forces that all serve to reinforce the expectations we place on individuals and legitimise their responsibility to lead. Distributed leadership challenges not only the authority of those in formal leader positions, but also their egos as well. As with all delegated or devolved activity, leaders become understandably vulnerable when they feel that their ability to control becomes threatened. It must also be said that subordinates also have expectations that leaders are always at the top of organisations and in control. In a review of the evidence, it has been suggested that it is better to think of distributed leadership as 'a way of thinking about leadership' rather than yet another leadership technique or practice.[43]

---

[42] Bennett *et al.* (2003), *op.cit.*

[43] Bennett *et al.* (2003), *op.cit.*, p.2.

We saw this new way of thinking as quite a challenge. We knew that the revival of the North could not rest with the individualised mentality of the past, whether we were concerned with leadership by single leaders or organisations such as universities, who could proclaim that they knew best. We saw our task as the spreading of influence through the practices of collaboration, collectivity and co-ordination, and these nicely matched recent concerns among the regional agencies for 'joined-up thinking', removal of fragmentation and business support simplification.[44] However, individuals, groups and organisations all work in their own interests, each driven forward but also constrained by ways of working deemed to be the path to success. History and culture play a vital role here and frequently can blind us to what we need to change. We saw a need for a radical critique of what has happened, opening up ideas and areas of activity that had been left or patched-over for years but were subtly, and sometimes cruelly, still exerting their influence and preventing progress. If, through our critique, we could construct a new story of what really works in leadership for SMEs and big business, local government, the public and voluntary services, then we could stretch the influence of that story right across the North. We needed to enact distributed leadership ourselves – collaborating, collectivising[45] and co-ordinating by creating mutually-beneficial networks of activity. We knew this would be a struggle – the weight of history was on our shoulders, but it was time to shrug it off!

To sum up: We see the appropriateness of distributed leadership in the North, due to the need to move towards a knowledge-based, high value-adding economic base, where people work interdependently, take joint responsibility for their performance and have a considerable degree of discretion over how work is carried out. These are also the features of the work of the NLA. We see the command and control notions of single agent leadership as obsolete. Attempts to retain such approaches by those in leadership positions will find themselves in confusion. As the poet W.B. Yeats once wrote:

---

[44]   These have been ongoing concerns of government too … go to http://www.dti.gov.uk
        /bbf/enterprise-smes/streamlining-government/bssp/page38586.html for details.

[45]   Clearly, by 'collectivising', we mean the creation of mutually-interdependent activities.

Things fall apart; the centre cannot hold;
Mere anarchy is loosed upon the world. [46]

The reason for such possibilities rests with the movement of work towards more discretion by staff, more interdependence between individuals and groups and the need for joint responsibility. In these situations, leadership occurs through the performance of work practices in response to local and situated influences exerted. Increasingly, in such work, and in our work in the NLA, different specialisms are required, which in turn requires interdependent relations so that specialisms can be integrated. This means local meanings, reciprocity and the use of discretion among groups of individuals, who jointly co-ordinate their efforts and further spread the influence over others and more situations. Of course, those appointed as leaders still have a role to play but they cannot pretend to control events. The behaviour of one person or group sets off a chain of reactions or new actions that is not subject to one person's control. There are potentially many voices that can exert an influence. Indeed, in the NLA, we seek to engender such a chain in the cause of the revival of the North through leadership and enterprise.

---

[46] From *The Second Coming* by W.B. Yeats, the first verse of which reads: 'Turning and turning in the widening gyre / The falcon cannot hear the falconer; / Things fall apart; the centre cannot hold; / Mere anarchy is loosed upon the world, / The blood-dimmed tide is loosed, and everywhere / The ceremony of innocence is drowned; / The best lack all convictions, while the worst / Are full of passionate intensity'.

PART 2:
PRINCIPLES OF GOOD PRACTICE

5

'LEADERFUL' COMMUNITIES

This chapter explains the vision of the Northern Leadership Academy (NLA), as it started its work.

We indicate the drive towards a new paradigm of 'leaderful' communities, which represent a step-change in understanding, which in turn requires a challenge to the traditional view of leaders as 'heroic'.

We look towards a view that sees leadership as more of a collective endeavour, shared between all who share a common sense of direction and know-how to influence those who have the authority, make decisions and act.

MECHANISMS FOR SUPPORTING & PROMOTING LEADERSHIP

The Northern Leadership Academy's vision is for a diverse, enterprising, pro-active community of leaders that becomes self-sustaining and growing, becoming a social and entrepreneurial magnet that will draw other talented individuals and investment to it.

Over two centuries after the Industrial Revolution, there was a need to rediscover the symbolic magnetism that drew people to the North. But, in the 21st century, there is a need to release and harness the talent of the many to deal with a more complex world, in contrast to the much simpler world of the 18th and 19th centuries, which could be changed by a relatively small number of inspired and inspiring entrepreneurs.

This did not mean providing yet more 'magic bullet' leadership courses that require participants to emulate heroes – only to fall at the first real hurdle back at work on Monday morning. The new perspective would reconnect leadership development with the everyday activities of leading. Rather than being distance learning, or traditional leadership development and executive education, the approach is 'close learning – learning that is embedded in local practice and relates closely to the needs of the person and the organisation in action.

We wanted the creation of sustainable communities, not unsustainable charismatics. That meant the need to distribute leadership in our community's collective and collaborative practices much more widely than before, because the challenges facing the North could not be resolved or transcended by a handful of gifted individuals.

TOWARDS A NEW PARADIGM OF
'LEADERFUL' COMMUNITIES

The conventional paradigm of leadership describes the heroic leader who is either 'born, not made' or, alternatively, selected then developed. We saw that a continuing over-emphasis on finding and developing heroic leaders would not solve the productivity problems of the North. Of course, appointed leaders and managers have a key role to play, but this is not the model of leadership that would transform the North. **Figure 5.1** summarises a vicious spiral of declining rates of productivity.

FIGURE 5.1: THE CONVENTIONAL PARADIGM OF THE HEROIC LEADER

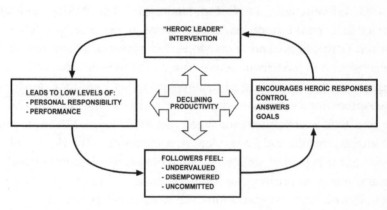

In its place, the NLA proposed a distributed view of leadership, where leaders can come from all walks of life, from all levels in organisations, and can be developed. Distributed leadership shifts people's mindsets, so that they assume individual and collective responsibility for their own and their organisation's development. People in leaderful organisations show their ingenuity, and offer solutions to organisational problems, supporting managers or CEOs in moving businesses forward, but who in turn responded by supporting and trusting their staff, feeding a spiral of improving productivity and growth (**Figure 5.2**).

FIGURE 5.2: THE NEW PARADIGM OF DISTRIBUTED LEADERSHIP

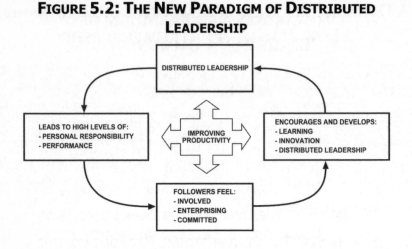

The NLA promoted distributed leadership, by making available demand-led, evidence-based development interventions that could transform business and enterprise, whether in large or small enterprises, or in the private or public sectors of the economy.

In effect, there was a need to re-create the culture that previously spawned entrepreneurial leaders in all areas of life, but on a much larger scale. It was these people who collectively created the industries, the schools and the public services that created the 'workshop of the world' and it is their inheritors that need to create the next equivalent. The aim has been nothing less than to create an inspiring community that individuals and organisations will want to belong to.

Thus, a precondition for (and then, a consequence of) the successful regeneration of the North is the construction and maintenance of an attractive regional identity – people must want to engage in this movement rather than be coerced or bribed into it. For this to underpin economic success, the vision of leaderful organisations and communities must be an inclusive one that emphasises how 'we' can achieve things to be proud of, rather than how much better we are than them (whoever 'they' are). If successful, this is a vision that will attract people who may not currently be part of the North, or feel Northern.

A DYNAMIC LEARNING PERSPECTIVE OF LEADERSHIP, MANAGEMENT & ENTREPRENEURSHIP

Organisations need management, entrepreneurship and leadership to succeed. But the division between them is more academic than real. In reality, the roles typically act simultaneously, suggesting the need for complementarities of development. The overlap of skills and competencies of entrepreneurship and leadership, for example, was a clear finding of the UK Government's Council for Excellence in Management & Leadership (CEML) in 2001, as illustrated in **Figure 5.3**.

FIGURE 5.3: THE OVERLAPPING COMPETENCIES OF LEADERSHIP & ENTREPRENEURSHIP

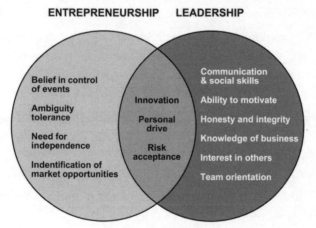

Source: Perren *et al.* (2001).

Entrepreneurship draws from management and leadership orientations and extends behaviour towards innovation, networking, visionary commitment and risk management. Rather than seeing entrepreneurship or leadership as inherited traits of a gifted few, the NLA has argued for a dynamic learning perspective that can be developed and supported over a lifetime and in different contexts. This perspective suggests that learning is critical to entrepreneurial effectiveness. It argues that the 'quest' for entrepreneurial personality and traits is over and that the focus has turned to understanding entrepreneurial processes, structures and contexts where learning can thrive.

The need to establish a more enterprising culture throughout the regions of the North was, and is, a common theme of the regional economic strategies (RES) of the three Regional Development Agencies (One NorthEast, Northwest Regional Development Agency and Yorkshire Forward) and is supported by their common emphasis on skills. Both factors are linked to the productivity issues raised by the substantial gap between the North and the UK as a whole. The RES documents also make clear the inter-relatedness of leadership and enterprise as co-factors needed to redress the gap.

The NLA promoted a view of leadership, management and entrepreneurship as something that can be fostered and encouraged to flourish in all sectors and all communities. The ability to enact this dynamic learning perspective had to be at the heart of the NLA, if it was to contribute to enhanced productivity through enterprising behaviour.

FROM VISION TO PRACTICE

Building from the value proposition and the vision for the NLA, there have been four linked activity areas seen as necessary to begin and advance our work:

1. A think-tank to provide the engine of thought leadership.
2. Evaluation, a very necessary process to gather evidence of what worked.
3. A web portal to disseminate good practice and to create a home for community activities.
4. Deliverables, pilot programmes to provide evidence.

Think-Tank

The purpose of the think-tank has been two-fold:

- Firstly, to see the direction of best practice principles through a critique of the direction taken through evaluation.
- Secondly, to provide an ongoing critique and review to allow for the emergence of new ideas and approaches, so direction can be adapted and changed.

These, in turn, provide further opportunities for exploitation.

The think-tank works as a creative dynamic of exploration, understanding, assessment and exploitation, a rich learning process and a cornerstone activity of the NLA, resulting in the development of key principles of what works for best practice leadership, management and enterprise development intervention.

Evaluation

Key to the provision of evidence is an evaluation service that provides insights into the stewardship of leadership development in the North. The principles of what works can be examined and developed in light of the continual evaluation process of the NLA, thereby creating a sustainable model of stewardship, updated through evidence-based evaluation, emerging research in the field of leadership and enterprise development.

Web portal

We established a new high-order virtual presence, a resource for dissemination and community linkage through a highly accessible integrated portal and virtual learning environment (VLE).

Deliverables

While not seeking to become a provider, the NLA nevertheless funded 26 pilot programmes to test the principles and build up evidence of what worked. These included SME mentoring cases, action learning sets with Sector Skills Councils, strategy master-classes, change conversations and community bridges. Each has been evaluated, adding to the flow of evidence to the think-tank in the build-up and refinement of principles of practice. They feature in some of the cases found in the chapters that follow.

6

SME PRINCIPLES & PROVISION

I n this chapter, we report the results of the
Northern Leadership Academy's work on
developing a set of principles that will guide the
practice of those involved in management and
leadership development within SMEs.

We claim no magic formula but, based on the research
evidence available, we argue that there are some
principles of good practice that can enhance
development and, in this chapter, we move the debate
on by showing how 'principles of good practice' can be
applied.

These principles have been developed from working
closely with SME managers and understanding the
world from their perspective. They offer the prospect of
changing the focus of both policy-makers and
practitioners alike.

INTRODUCTION

Whilst there has been a long-standing concern with 'a lack of leadership and inadequate management' within SMEs in the UK,[47] in recent years there has been an increasing agreement about what might be possible from those engaged in their development. The Council for Excellence in Management & Leadership, reporting in 2002, suggested the need to move away from the confusion of over-lapping agendas between Government Departments and a 'jumble of funding drivers', which resulted in an over-emphasis on the supply of SME learning and development opportunities, towards the stimulation of demand and the circumstances that might create demand. This view has most recently found favour in the findings of the 2006 Leitch[48] review of skill development, which seeks to shift power from suppliers to consumers in the market for skills. Nonetheless, it remains the case that most SMEs remain classified as hard-to-reach and 'tough nuts to crack', as though it is the SME managers that are guilty of neglect – and we know this is not the case!

While many SMEs undoubtedly benefit from management and leadership development, it is indisputable that SME managers often lack time to be able to lift their heads and think about anything other than operational activities. It is hardly surprising, therefore, that most learning in SMEs often takes place outside formal educational settings. What we know about SME managers is that they learn most about what they need to be able to manage from significant work-related experiences and that, although this learning happens naturally, learning can be enhanced if the learning opportunities can be structured and the events can be reflected upon critically and knowledge and information fed in a flexible way. We know, for example, that SME managers learn significantly from peers, customers and suppliers, and this learning is not recognised as learning by the managers themselves because it is part of everyday, valued interactions.

---

[47]   Patricia Hewitt, the then secretary of State for Trade & Industry, in her response to the report of the Council for Excellence in Management & Leadership, 13 May 2002.

[48]   Leitch, S. (2006). *Prosperity for All in the Global Economy – World Class Skills, Final report of the Leitch Review of Skills*, London: HMSO / HM Treasury.

When it comes to the issue of appropriate provision of management and leadership learning activities, one crucial factor is the disposition that managers have towards the growth and performance of the organisation. It has been recognised consistently that most SME managers are not concerned with growth, but rather with survival. As a consequence of their size and inability to affect their circumstances, they lack the capability to plan strategically, or reflect on the ways in which their businesses might develop. Recent evidence relating to the measurement of performance in SMEs appears to confirm this situation. It has been found that lack of time for anything other than operational activities stops a move to more long-term orientation and the adoption of more systemic measures of performance like Gross Value Added or Balanced Scorecard indicators.

FIGURE 6.1: MOVING FROM SHORT-TERM OPERATIONAL VIEWS & MEASURES TOWARDS LONGER-TERM STRATEGIC MEASURES & PERSPECTIVES

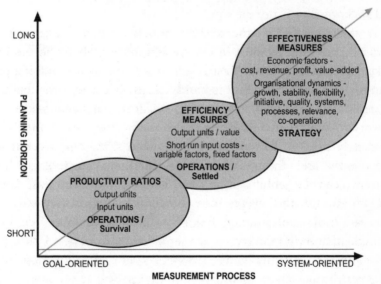

Figure 6.1 illustrates how the short-term performance measures often used by (or forced on) managers of small firms need to be broadened out to be more systems-based, if growth and development is to take place. In terms of the diagram this means moving from a position

where many firms begin, the bottom left (where the measures used are partial and short-term – for example, turnover), towards the top right, where the measures used give information that might question the whole nature of the business model (where the performance of the whole organisation is measured – for example, return on capital employed or added value).

To collect such data requires managers to be able to stand back from the hurly-burly of the day-to-day; to do this, they need to be able to create 'space' for themselves, so that they can think ahead and reflect on the context of the business and the opportunities for change.

This shortage of time to undertake a proper analysis of performance, even if models are employed, usually means implementation tends to be incomplete or incorrect. Growth, therefore, in the SME sector is seen mostly from the perspective of capital growth and / or employment generation, which can be inappropriate and misplaced, if managers wish to consolidate their businesses and, instead of growing into large oak trees, just wish to be little bonsais and survive.

A recent piece of research,[49] conducted in the North-west of England, has been helpful in our understanding about how owner-managers lead their firms through crises, and manage to adopt a more strategic orientation. This research focuses particularly on how informal learning, past experiences, systems and engagement with others are central to this strategic learning process, but that actual practices between firms differ. In other words, the research suggests that it is not the adoption of 'best practice' that is the key to a firm's success. A firm's actual learning and leadership activities are largely unique, but, where they are most successful is when they create the resources, time and 'strategic space'[50] to lift their attention towards a more distant horizon. Effective managers are able to stand back from day-to-day activities and consider longer-term issues which impact on their businesses. The following section discusses this research in more detail.

---

[49] ESRC Project Report RES 334-25-0015. An account of the research is presented in Thorpe, R., Jones, O., Macpherson, A & Holt, R. (2008). 'The evolution of business knowledge in SMEs', Scarbrough, H. (ed.). *The Evolution of Business Knowledge*, Oxford: Oxford University Press.

[50] Jones, O., Macpherson, A., Thorpe, R. & Ghecham A. (2007). 'The evolution of business knowledge in SMEs: Conceptualising strategic space', *Journal of Strategic Change* 16(6): 281-294.

THE EVOLUTION OF BUSINESS KNOWLEDGE IN SMALLER FIRMS[51]

SMEs make a significant contribution to the UK economy and provide the majority, about 56%, of all private sector jobs. Despite this contribution, it is surprising that we still know relatively little about the management processes in smaller firms. While we know a lot about large organisations, SMEs are different. SMEs have many features that distinguish them from their large firms – for example:

- Absence of formal structure.
- Dominance of owner-managers.
- Lack of internal labour markets
- Environmental uncertainty.
- Limited customer base.

Practices appropriate for large firms may not necessarily work in a small firm. The inherent flexibility and informality of SMEs, coupled with a view that they are defined very much by the personal commitment of their owners, means that they are likely to be shaped by the owners, through their responses to perceptions of existing organisational conditions (markets, skills, opportunities, etc). These perceptions then are translated into actions to define organisational conditions, routines and processes. We thus recognise that the evolution of a small firm is likely to be influenced by the development of firm-based resources and capabilities, through a range of activities, rather than the accrual of knowledge resources. Thus, our research is less concerned with understanding data acquisition and more interested in understanding how and why an owner adopts a particular set of organisational practices.

With these concerns in mind, this study (which commenced in 2003) was designed to develop an understanding of how owner-managers dealt with 'critical incidents', such as a financial crisis, losing staff or acquiring new customers. Of particular interest was the way in which such critical incidents led to the acquisition of new knowledge and the development of learning processes within the SME. The study

---

[51]   A research project funded by the Economic & Social Research Council.

engaged 90 SMEs in the North-west of England, operating in three sectors:

- Services (media and culture and retail).
- Client-based (bespoke advice and formulaic advice).
- Manufacturing (high-tech and low-tech).

The firms also varied according to their level of business maturity: start-up, stable and innovatory.

Research involved interviews over 18 months and more in-depth case studies with 12 firms. Our findings confirmed that most of the SMEs were reactive in their responses to external change and typified by high levels of informality. However, the findings also suggested that this informality, while it could be an important source of competitive advantage, could serve also to inhibit the acquisition and embedding of new knowledge.

RESULTS

Analysis of the interview transcripts and case studies identified four areas of particular importance for the evolution of knowledge.

The first identified the importance of formal systems, procedures and routines by which new knowledge could be embedded. Too much reliance on informality means there are no mechanisms for sharing and retaining knowledge. Second, these systems can provide triggers that stimulate discussion and debate leading to the generation of new knowledge. It was not the introduction of the Balanced Scorecard or the Business Excellence model *per se*, but rather the debate, which implementation of these processes engendered, that was important. New systems and routines create discussions and / or a review of existing practices. In turn, this enables owner-managers to free themselves to debate longer-term issues with other stakeholders.

The third and fourth factors relate to sources of innovation (new products, services and processes) reliant on owner-managers' human capital. Human capital is represented partly by their education, but, perhaps more importantly, by their experience, attitude and ability to make sense of the challenges they face in the context of their experiences. This ability to formulate a view, often in complex and ambiguous situations, was embodied in their 'discursive resources': their ability to communicate effectively with a wide range of stakeholders (employees, customers, suppliers, financiers, etc). These abilities were linked to social skills and social capital, through which owner-managers developed relationships, through which in turn they encouraged others to engage with their projects. For example, effective owner-managers have the ability and vision to bridge into new networks when they require additional resources such as knowledge and information, the 'maturity' to forge their own path despite pressures to do otherwise, and / or the ability to delegate and encourage others to participate in their venture. These four issues are discussed in detail below.

Knowledge systems

Our findings support the received wisdom in relation to larger organisations, in that the involvement of customers and extensive prior experience were both important in learning. Additionally, we found that, where owner-managers have diverse skills and used relatively-sophisticated management techniques, they made stronger performance claims. However, there was little focus on the acquisition and use of knowledge as a linear, causal process. Instead, accounts were of experiential knowledge acquisition through fragile, fragmentary and confused processes. Outcomes were often the adoption of new systems and processes (formal or informal) that helped to retain and distribute knowledge throughout the firm. Often the systems were idiosyncratic and personalised – for example, a chalk line drawn onto a wall, suggesting in particular the importance of informal approaches.

Similarly, knowledge-sharing was often problematic. It is particularly dependent on the ability of the owner-manager to institutionalise new practices throughout the firm, otherwise learning is limited to the few who negotiate and resolve problems in a particular setting. Where learning was distributed more effectively, owner-managers recognised that, when acquiring and using knowledge, it was more important to create a forum for debate and to involve others in the process. Embedding knowledge, either formally or informally, in the systems of day-to-day work, and involving others in the development of those systems, allowed the firm to adopt new practices quickly.

Conversational space and boundary objects

The fact that many owner-managers had little time and were reactive was not a surprise. What was important was the quality of the relationships that owner-managers developed, not the number of their contacts. For example, ISO 9000 was often used as a tool and as an 'artefact' or 'object', around which individuals could discuss alternative approaches. Value was created where outside influence – for example, working with professional advisers – guided rather than dictated conversation. These objects, such as ISO 9000, Balanced Scorecard, or other business analysis tools, act as a way of abstracting and representing understanding, but they also stimulate discussion and debate. In other words, they also have the potential to stimulate learning. For this to happen, there needed to be commitment to new activities, at the heart of which lay communication and engagement and a willingness to change. In order to understand the construction and transformation of knowledge within SMEs, it is important to attend to both 'spaces' and 'objects' and associated social practices. Moreover, it was noted that outside agencies, such as academic institutions, customers, suppliers or professional advisers, can influence these conversations and debates, creating the sort of conversational space and objects around which learning can be stimulated and accelerated to encourage the institutionalisation of new activities.

Social competence

One sub-study, focusing on three owner-managers, suggested that the effective use of knowledge was dependent on their ability to create 'rhetorical rapport' between themselves and their audience. This social skill allowed owner-managers to engage more effectively with customers, employees and interviewers. The successful organisation of activity (in our three chosen cases, these were: a move of premises; an attempt to involve suppliers in working practices; and a change to shift patterns) relied significantly on the ability of owner-managers to convince others that their vision and strategies were legitimate and important for success.

Our analysis of their narrative accounts shows how, despite the privileged role they each held within their organisation, when they had to respond to the inherent ambiguity that crises create, managing that change effectively meant that they had to convince others based on appeals of simple economic logic. Successful change also involved owner-managers attending to their own credibility (were they figures of trust?) and to the perspective of their audience (how would new practices, ways of working, etc. affect their jobs, markets or products?). In other words, what was important was the owner-managers social competence to engage with, and excite, others' interest, to align interests towards their venture.

The importance of social capital

The final finding relates to how business networks and professional advisers were influential within dynamic firms. They were used as significant sources of new knowledge. In addition, recruitment of senior managers is important because they bring in new human and social capital and allow the delegation of responsibilities. The recruitment of new staff also increased social capital, since they brought with them their own network of contacts. It was clear that the awareness owner-managers had about the creation and destruction of social capital through social relations was important to success, and is clearly linked to the notion of social competence above.

Our findings suggest that there are a variety of network relationships that can enable and constrain social capital. Success in doing so relies on social skills, awareness of the potential usefulness of contacts and the motivation to engage with others. The opposite is also evident. We noted that a lack of social capital and a lack of ability or motivation to extend networks was a source of frustration. Owner-managers need *both* the social skills and the time (or space) to do this. The importance of space and interaction has been noted above, but here we are more concerned with the agency and structure of social capital through which knowledge is renewed.

Modelling the evolution of business knowledge

Figure 6.2 represents an acknowledgement that human capital (incorporating sense-making and discursive resources) is the key influence on SMEs' social capital and knowledge systems.

FIGURE 6.2: MEANS BY WHICH STRATEGIC SPACE IS CREATED

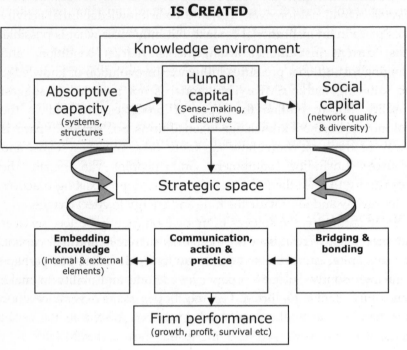

Source: Jones *et al.* (2007).

Hence, knowledge and knowing are embedded within the structures and relationships that exist within the firm's sphere of influence. Also, this knowledge capacity is renewed though interaction, engagement and activities that, in part, are structured by existing social relationships and structures. In order for knowledge renewal to take place, 'strategic space' has to be created to allow existing activities or 'objects' to be put under review. By strategic space, we mean the time, resources, motivation and capabilities – so that owner-managers have the opportunity to reflect on, and review, existing organisational practices. At the heart of learning and knowledge renewal in small firms are the actions and practices that encourage communication. It is these practices that require time and space, so that owner-managers can bridge into communities of suppliers, customers and within their own firms and create a bond, a shared sense of the project. For responses to particular crises to be effective, ultimately there has to be the institutionalisation and embedding of new knowledge into new *collective* activities. Moreover, it should be acknowledged that activity takes place in an institutional context that influences what is possible. Thus, current institutional arrangements, market conditions and changing institutional pressures influence the evolution of knowledge and knowing within SMEs. This model is not intended to suggest causality, but to outline the types of processes involved in the evolution of business knowledge in small firms. So, 'strategic space' is a way of thinking about how a variety of activities, systems, and resources (including equipment and people) can create the opportunity to raise the horizons of practice, to put existing practices under review and to provide the time and energy to effect change.

So, in summary, the sources of innovation (new products, services and processes) were reliant on the owner-managers' human capital. Human capital is represented partly by their education, but perhaps more importantly by their experience, attitude and ability to make sense of the challenges they face in the context of the experiences they have had. These abilities we also found were linked to the social capital available *via* various network relationships to the SME.

The second factor that distinguished high performance SMEs was their knowledge systems, what is called 'absorptive capacity'.[52] We found that it was crucial for SMEs to have formal systems, procedures and routines, by which new knowledge could be embedded within the firm. Too much reliance on informality means there are no mechanisms for sharing and retaining knowledge. We also found that the systems themselves provided an important trigger to stimulate discussion and debate and, through this, the generation of new knowledge. So, for many, it was not the fact that they had introduced a new system that was important. It was the debate, which the implementation of new systems engendered, that provided opportunities to learn anew about the business and its potential. Perhaps more than anything though, it was 'space' that systems or routines created, which provided the manager with time and motivation to consider the longer term, that was the key to performance improvement, rather than the system itself.

---

[52]   Cohen, W.M. & Levinthal, D.A. (1990). 'Absorptive capacity: A new perspective on learning and innovation', *Administrative Science Quarterly* 35(1): 128-52.

IMPLICATIONS

The findings from this research have some significant implications for SME managers and policy-makers. First, we found it crucial that owner-managers are able to create the kinds of 'strategic space' highlighted above, by delegating responsibility within the firm and 'opening-up' to external sources of advice and information. Secondly, learning within the firm can be much more effective if it is problem-centred and learner-centred and incorporates 'boundary objects' (such as business analysis tools, problem-solving forums or soft-process technologies) to assist the process of engagement and dialogue between staff at all levels. Thirdly, we thought it was important that Government agencies and funding bodies move away from classifying SMEs simply in terms of size (number of employees or turnover and so on) and, instead, focus more on the owner-manager's human and social capital and the firm's absorptive capacity, as it is firms with higher levels of potential absorptive capacity that are far more likely to respond positively to external advice and support.

The impact of our study has already been felt in the way it has informed the principles of leadership being established by the Northern Leadership Academy. The NLA is being funded by the three RDAs in the North and is a partnership of universities to support and stimulate leadership and its development across the north of England, in order close the productivity gap and raise levels of performance. The study findings have enabled us to consider how we might communicate and engage with users, providers and policy-makers more effectively, in order to improve firm performance and, where appropriate, facilitate delivery on the ground.

The NLA currently is developing a number of programmes to stimulate SME development, which will be delivered throughout the North. These programmes will serve to distribute 'good practice' and to build capacity in the delivery of entrepreneurship and leadership. We also plan to develop a number of 'hubs' that will provide some physical 'spaces', where managers and teams can meet and be encouraged to think more strategically about their firms' development needs and possibilities.

LEARNING TO LEAD A SMALL BUSINESS

Traditionally, learning is understood in psychological and behavioural terms concerning changes in behaviour due to some experience or activity. Crucially, such changes need to be permanent, and seen by others to have occurred. Of course, traditionally, classroom-based education and training courses are based on this idea, which suggests that, if learning has occurred, then we should be able to measure its effects. Furthermore, its suggests that the conditions and experiences of the learner can be adjusted and manipulated, so as to ensure that individuals and groups show the desired behaviour changes.

However, this view of learning evidently ignores the role of an individual's thoughts about the experience and his / her interactions with groups and sees the learner as an unsuspecting and unthinking being, ready to be changed in whatever way is deemed desirable by the 'educator'.

In a similar way, models of management development have tended to be divided into those that concentrate on the individual and those that focus on the organisation. Many of the models emphasise that management development is a deliberate and planned activity and something that is done to managers. Models of management education, when managers go to college for qualifications such as MBAs, similarly cast the manager as the receiver of knowledge rather than an active participant in its formation and use. This dominant image of the manager then is as a passive participant in the learning process and someone rather marginal, as opposed to a person central, active and integrated.

Other approaches provide a more accessible framework for those involved in SME owner-manager development, especially those that consider learners as more mature and already with experience to draw upon. These approaches make rather different assumptions about the way adults learn:[53]

- **The need to know:** Adult learners need to know why they need to learn something before undertaking to learn it.

---

[53]   We have adapted these from the work of Knowles, M. (1990). *The Adult Learner: A Neglected Species,* Houston: Gulf Publishing Co.

- **Learner self-concept:** Adults need to be responsible for their own decisions and to be treated as capable of self-direction.

- **Role of learners' experience:** Adult learners have a variety of experiences of life that represent the richest resource for learning. However, these experiences are imbued with bias and presupposition.

- **Readiness to learn:** Adults are ready to learn those things they need to know in order to cope effectively with life situations.

- **Orientation to learning:** Adults are motivated to learn, to the extent that they perceive that it will help them perform tasks they confront in their life situations.

These points begin to move our attention away from the traditional passive models of learning, which suggest the learner is a container waiting to be filled, and put emphasis on learning that is informal, more natural and that occurs every day. There is now a growing appreciation that a manager's learning takes place as a consequence of their everyday activities and interactions.[54] This recognition chimes with associated research into management and leadership learning more generally, where informal learning is predominant over formal processes. As a consequence, there is a move towards designs of working with managers that reflect better the informal processes of learning they favour. This also provides a better opportunity to help managers challenge some of the constraints they face that prevent them and their organisations from making progress.

This can involve helping managers to become more reflective and more critical about the views they hold and the practices they adopt. Here, the distinction between single-loop and double-loop learning is useful.[55] Single-loop learning occurs when experiences are interpreted according to currently-held views and expectation. There is no challenge to existing thoughts and meanings, just a means of adjustment of thoughts in line with those meanings. For example, if finances are judged according to simple bottom-line criteria, single-

---

[54] This is even acknowledged by the Confederation of British Industry in a recent publication, *Informality Works*, published in 2003.

[55] This distinction is based on the work of Chris Argyris, in his book, *Reasons & Rationalisations: the Limits to Organisational Knowledge*, published in 2004 by Oxford University Press.

loop learning would be concerned with how to restore a satisfactory bottom-line position where this was not happening. Double-loop learning requires a reinterpretation of such meanings. So, while simple bottom-line measures are important, perhaps they are also limiting and other measures can be considered that may help the business expand in the future. Without help, managers normally would stay safe with single-loop learning and double-loop learning is not the everyday 'stuff' of experiential learning. Even when, through natural experiences triggered by everyday events, there is potential for double-loop learning, the learning is usually limited to the instant needs of the moment and so is highly perishable. What is recalled for later use is rarely retained for use outside of its context. SME managers need to be helped to learn beyond their instant requirement for practical action. To achieve this, it appears that reflection, and particularly critical reflection, becomes significantly important.

All this needs to occur in the place where it is relevant to the manager, usually at work or in a context supportive of change. Of great importance are the relationships between persons and activities where thoughts, ideas and knowledge are transferred and leads to action. Of significance to SME managers is the fact that they are usually at the hub of their organisations. In addition, they are instrumental in the creation of practices, situations and meanings that are at the heart of what is learnt. In essence, through their own learning at work in their own community of practice, that they can become the 'glass ceiling' for growth and learning. The provision of complementary communities with alternative relationships thus are of significant importance.

Similarly important and central to such learning is the process of how managers come to understand themselves and their organisation. Through the relationships of the SME managers with employees, family, customers and suppliers, the identity and associated practice of the manager is shaped. These identities again have been seen to limit learning and development of managers greatly.

Any intervention to influence practice and identity must take account of the communities of practice in which it takes place. As a consequence, interventions need to consider the story of the situation that links informal and natural learning to the process of knowledge acquisition and processes of becoming part of a particular way of life, indeed the 'world' they call their organisation.

These ideas about SME learning are also evident when we consider entrepreneurs. There is rich literature around entrepreneurial learning, that is those who start and grow their own businesses. In fact, many businesses now exhort their employees to be more entrepreneurial, encompassing the idea of someone who is innovative, willing to take risks, is creative and has a vision of the future. So whilst many managers, in the strictest sense, may not be entrepreneurs, many of them feel the need to develop these skills (or qualities) in order to be successful (in whatever context this is understood)

FRAMEWORKS FOR ENTREPRENEURIAL LEARNING IN SMEs

One framework for entrepreneurial learning consists of a model with three major themes:[56]

- Identity.
- Contextual learning.
- Negotiated enterprise.

The first theme of entrepreneurial identity includes:

- Narrative construction of identity.
- Identity as practice.
- Their role in relation to their family.
- Tension between current and future identity.

Contextual learning allows entrepreneurs to recognise and act on emergent opportunities and includes:

- Learning through immersion within the industry or community.
- Opportunity recognition through cultural participation.
- Practical theories of entrepreneurial action.

---

[56] We base this on the work of David Rae in 'Entrepreneurial learning: A practical model from the creative industries', published in 2004 in *Education & Training*.

The third theme of the negotiated enterprise includes:

- Participation and joint enterprise.
- Negotiated meaning, structures and practices.
- Engagement in networks of external relationships.
- Changing roles over time.

This framework provides us with a model of how the entrepreneur learns from experience and from reflecting on that experience. It provides a set of reflective questions that acts as an 'educational aid' – the sense-making process that may lead to 'transformative' learning.

These ideas provide us with the 'learning' basis for our principles for SME leadership and management development;. This work is coalesced and extended to produce the set of principles discussed below. It is intended for use by providers and evaluators of management and leadership development in the SME sector.

We discuss each of the seven principles in turn. Each principle is stated in italics, followed by our discussion. We end each discussion with a number of key questions that could be used to consider projects for working with SME leaders and managers.

1. Engage with the identity and interests of the manager

For managers in SMEs, learning becomes meaningful when it is strongly related to their concerns, problems and desires. It is important to explore the situation they are in and how this has come about. Every manager will have a story of who they are, how they come to be where they are and, possibly, what they are trying to achieve. The organisations they manage and lead are something that they personally value, both emotionally and financially. There may also be a long history to their position and this needs to be appreciated. Abstract concepts are unhelpful, if they do not form part of the sense-making activities that help managers and relate to the image of themselves as leaders. SME managers are often very sceptical, if not cynical, about outside help and certainly they are sensitive to exposing potential 'weakness'. Therefore, it is fundamental to gain confidence, mutual respect and trust, as well as to establish perspective and relativity.

Small business growth is linked intrinsically to the growth and development of the manager. Their identity as a manager and the self-confidence associated with success in owning and running a business is socially constituted. SME managers often choose to set up their businesses because they are disenchanted with the depersonalising effects of working in other, particularly large, organisations. An entrepreneurial identity, for example, emerges through the formation of a sense of self and of future aspirations; entrepreneurs may seek to renegotiate or 're-invent' their identities as they set up and grow their enterprise. This creation of a new identity often occurs through autobiographical stories, in which they are placed as the central character. The process of the creation of self can be contrasted with the process by which a manager in a large organisation undergoes; the importance of being, or becoming, a member of a management profession and the identity work involved in that is negligible or non-existent until the business and its systems grow. SME managers may also have difficulty in separating personal and business issues. Their prominent role means that issues affecting them in their personal lives often seem to have a potent effect on business activities and, ultimately, on the success of the organisation.

Key questions to consider for engagement with the identity and interests of the manager:

- Is there a process to engage hard-to-reach managers?
- How are concerns, problems and desires identified?
- Are the situation and the history of that situation explored?
- How is the manager's story accessed?
- Is the next stage of that story in evidence?
- Is there an opportunity for managers to explain their personal interest?

2. Understand the context and build from it

The lived experience of the SME manager both shapes, and is shaped by, the context of the organisation, so it is important to understand this context before any activity can be provided. The particular context of the organisation and the issues arising from it provides the reality that the managers must face and any development must connect with it. The 'best practice' approaches of leadership development in larger organisations start from the wrong premise. For many SME managers, the desire to be self-employed greatly shapes their disposition to learning. SME managers have to establish 'balance' between strategic and operational performance, as well as between management and leadership. However, through their experiences of running their business, themes of loneliness and isolation are common. They have a desire to understand whether the way they run their businesses is appropriate. While this potentially opens a possibility to explore new ideas, there must be connection to the realities they face.

Understanding, acknowledging and working within the context of the organisation is key to the success of development interventions in the SME sector. We need to emphasise the importance of recognising the differences between large and small employers and firms operating in different sectors and markets. We know that, in micro and small businesses, interest and usage rates of Government training initiatives amongst managers usually is low, confirming the assertion that traditional management development objectify and decontextualise learning. The diverse nature of the SME sector also means that different skills and competences are needed from business to business, and at different stages of the firm's development.

Key questions to consider to facilitate a greater understanding of the context and the ability to build from it:

- How are the context and history explored and assessed?
- How are the key issues facing the manager diagnosed and assessed?
- How is a baseline for improvement established?
- What is the connection of development to the issues faced?
- How will success be understood?
- What approach to learning is preferred and how is this assessed?
- What is the potential for new ideas that connect to the context and issues faced?

3. Respond to the time-frame as appropriate

It is important to understand an SME manager's thinking about time-frames. The reality is that most SMEs have extremely short planning horizons and order books that barely last more than one or two months at a time. Indeed, SMEs that operate at survival levels work with a time-frame that can best be summarised as 'here and now'. Thus, strategy development and long-term business growth, more often than not, are relegated to the background or do not feature at all in the 'thinking' of SMEs. For such managers, attempts to move too quickly beyond immediate concerns are likely to be rejected. However, recent research has shown that there is a significant association between a SME's approach to strategic planning and its business performance and those that engage in a 'strategic' approach to their organisations, working with time-frames from one to five years, are likely to be more profitable with a greater capacity to grow, innovate and develop new products.

For a variety of reasons, SME managers are compelled to remain reactive and *ad hoc* in their approach to strategic work, although there is considerable evidence that, if a longer view can be taken and strategic planning embraced, growth becomes more likely. Indeed, it is suggested that any strategy that involves some degree of future thinking is an advance on nothing at all. CEML took witness accounts from entrepreneurs and SME managers and found a key difference between them to be the emphasis on strategic / analytical thinking abilities given by entrepreneurs. This connects strongly to evidence on innovation, growth and knowledge generation in SMEs, where there is a need to 'create space' and to build the opportunity to allow an effective and innovative use of knowledge.

Key questions to consider in order to respond to the time-frame as appropriate:

- How is the manager's thinking on time-frames considered?
- How important are immediate concerns to the manager?
- How will development work with time-frames?
- What provision is there for movement in thinking about time-frames?
- Can thinking become more strategic?

---

4. Determine the measurement and what is valued

How SMEs measure their performance is strongly connected to the response managers have to what they learn. The measures managers use can constrain and limit learning, especially as research suggests that most SMEs find it difficult to participate in performance measurement projects because of the lack of time available for anything other than operational activities. Further performance measurement is narrowly focused, usually on financial and operational aspects, with little awareness for integration or systemic consideration. Even where a performance model is employed, the implementation tends to be partial or incorrect – a consequence perhaps of most models being more suited to larger organisations. Measurement is not planned but is responsive to, and emerges from, solving problems, the consequence of which is that any measures that do emerge are past-oriented and developed to support control.

Many SME managers concentrate on the 'here and now', finding it impossible to plan ahead or envision the future. Many are 'hands-on' operational managers by necessity; spending time solving problems and making decisions that only they can deal with. We also need to be aware that SME managers do not understand success in the same way as it might be represented in other organisations (both large and small). There is some evidence of definitions of success, as offered by managers themselves rather than merely using externalised measures such as the profitability, growth or sustainability of the business, being growth and profitability achieved through a work philosophy based on teamwork. For others, success might be enjoyment by being happy at work and ensuring staff and customers enjoy their experiences. Then there are those who see success in terms of a sense of achievement by creating a shared vision and a collective sense of achievement, or simply achievement and recognition.[57]

If success is perceived in a range of different ways, then the impact of training and development interventions will be extremely difficult to measure in the same way each time or with one dimension of measurement. Providers and researchers need to look beyond formal measures when assessing the impact of training initiatives in the SME sector.

Key questions to consider in order to determine the measurement of what is valued:

- How is the manager's thinking on time-frames considered?
- How important are immediate concerns to the manager?
- How will development work with time-frames?
- What provision is there for movement in thinking about time-frames?
- Can thinking become more strategic?

---

[57]   We have derived these views from the work of Mike Simpson, Nicki Tuck and Sarah Bellamy in their article, 'Small business success factors: The role of education and training', published in *Education & Training* in 2004.

5. Stimulate entrepreneurship and stretch

SME managers generally are concerned with present interests, seeking to provide repairs or improvements to current ways of working. It is important to assess existing capacity and capabilities and to explore the potential for making an advance. Each manager will have a meaning for such advances, simultaneously providing the potential and limit for development. Attempting to move the manager too far beyond this point will be seen as inappropriate or unrealistic. However, over time, and through the development of relationships with others, it may become possible to gain command of new capabilities, setting a new and higher limit on the potential and limit for development.

When CEML declared that, on the basis of the existing supply-led provision and the absence of 'demand-led' solutions, there was a need to 'join the entrepreneur in their own world' so that provision reflected personal aspirations and ambitions, this immediately raised issues concerning the nature of the SME world and how it might be understood. Given the vast number of business organisations that can be categorised as SMEs, it is not surprising that there have not yet been any significant advances in providing a fully-worked-out response to such issues. Nevertheless, as CEML identified, failure to engage with SMEs in their world is unlikely to lead to effective management and leadership development.

There is a need to more consider each SME manager as a separate case, each with his / her own story, history and valued direction. We suggest this can be achieved by understanding the uniqueness of SMEs and the workings of processes in a particular time and place that give rise to the manager's version of reality. It is these local versions of reality that make the SME world, and set the limits of what is possible. Any attempt to move beyond such limits is likely to be rejected. Nevertheless, by sensitive consideration of the peculiarities of the manager's understanding of reality, new ideas can be introduced to stimulate movements and to challenge the limits that are usually self-imposed. Successful completions of new activities allows the making of new meanings and new realities that expand the limits of the SME world.

Key questions to consider in order to stimulate entrepreneurship and stretch:

- How are existing capacity and capabilities assessed?
- What are the meanings given by the manager for advance and progress?
- How will goals set be appropriate to the manager?
- How will new goals enable the development of new capabilities?

6. Develop communities of practice

Learning by managers in SMEs most often occurs naturally by completing work and solving problems as part of an everyday process. Such learning is the by-product of a work process, rather than the focus of the process itself, and is shared with everyone involved in the process. The accumulation of such learning over time, and the meanings attached to what is done, become accepted by everyone connected to the organisation. SME managers also like to learn with, and from, others who have similar concerns and face similar issues. There is a need for learning to connect to action; being able to consider the possibilities with others who can understand the realities they face is more likely to lead to success. The social and interdependent dimension of learning therefore is crucial. Through conversations, during which managers share information, seek help and generally give meaning to their work, collective knowledge is created that enables, sustains, constrains but also advances its practice.

Most SME managers have their own network of relationships that they maintain for guidance and help. This network has a crucial role to play in learning, for good or ill. The network provides specific social contexts for a manager's action, and the knowledge acquired in these contexts are more meaningful than abstract theories found in books or journals. For new ideas to be considered, a context where there is sufficient shared understanding and common experiences provides a more positive likelihood of acceptance. SME managers like to learn from people who are like them. This is both enabling, in the sense of building connections, but constraining in setting limits on what can be learnt. Prescriptions imposed by others on the outside pay no attention to the fact that managers cannot always speak and act as they please, in which understanding, describing and solving problems are all achieved through dialogue within their communities.

Key questions to consider in order to develop communities of practice:

- What are the opportunities for managers to learn with others who face similar issues?
- How will learning connect to action at work?
- How will learning consider others who have an interest and role in action at work?
- Can action taken be reviewed with others?
- Will there be space for managers to have conversations between themselves?

---

7. Enhance belief, confidence and awareness

Any attempt to provide support for SME management and leadership development requires a space to attract managers into a conversation. Development interventions must recognise the need for appropriate language, appropriate learning contexts (often their context and other businesses) and a pedagogy premised on exchanges of experiences and ideas. There is the need to help managers identify how interventions relate to their business, how this helps the development of both the business and themselves, from which they can aspire to an appropriate identity. A key characteristic of this approach is the extent to which managers are able to set the agenda and influence the direction and speed of conversations, according to their own interests, gaining confidence as they do so. Similarly, there is a need to reinforce the identity development process by focusing on areas of competence and skill development.

Learners who are confident are able to set and achieve ambitious goals. 'Successful' entrepreneurs and managers have high levels of self-belief, which in turn, feeds self-confidence and creates a virtuous cycle of learning. This focus on the manager as a confident and dynamic individual reflects the stereotypical view of the proactive entrepreneur. However, the principles that we are creating and have been working with in the Northern Leadership Academy are meant not only for those managers who display the archetypal entrepreneurial skill-set but for the whole range of SME leaders. Self-confidence can be engendered and developed in a range of ways dependent on the need of the individual, heroically entrepreneurial or not. So learning must include some element of being self-directed and be appropriately personalised to managers needs.

Key questions to consider in order to enhance belief, confidence and awareness:

- Is there scope for critique and raising awareness of new possibilities?
- Is challenge supported?
- Are new or different perspectives available for consideration?
- Can new or different perspectives lead to change in practice?
- Can changes be reviewed for impact and learning?

SUMMARY

Most agencies currently involved in the provision of SME growth and development programmes are preoccupied with the notion of ending supply-driven activity and concentrating on demand- or market-driven activity; the idea that we should 'join them (SME owner-managers) in their worlds'. In this chapter, we have attempted to articulate and discuss how we might better understand how SME managers learn and are motivated to continue learning, as a way of devising and delivering demand-driven development and growth programmes. This market-driven approach often is conceptualised as simply the antithesis of supply-driven initiatives. However, this over-simplification belies the depth of understanding of the real drivers and motivators for learning (and of course, an understanding of the demotivating factors), which is required to engage managers in taking responsibility for their own learning and to profit truly from the range of initiatives on offer to them.

The principles we have developed here have been part of our endeavours during the two years of working in the Northern Leadership Academy. They were developed partly in response to various partners, who sought advice on how to make progress on the SME management and leadership 'problem'. The principles reflect what we consider to be findings from the evidence of various sources. However, while they provide some light, they still do not penetrate the apparent darkness, in terms of our understanding of the valued realities and interests of the many SME managers. Principles are another form of abstraction, a decontextualisation from the realities we seek to understand. Therefore, it is important to work with partners to create further understanding of how the principles play out in practice. Indeed, to that extent, we and our partners must consider our principles reflexively and critically.

7

ESTABLISHING DEMAND
IN SMEs

I n this chapter, we argue that the stimulation of demand for development is largely concerned with getting close enough to managers and leaders so that their problems can be understood properly and expressed in terms that make sense to them in their terms and in their contexts.

We go on to suggest that this understanding then opens the door for development opportunities. Crucial here is the way that solutions to problems can be attempted and completed by the leader at a level beyond which he / she would be capable of alone. Through a series of successful completions and 'quick-wins', relationships can be built and a path for future development established.

At the heart of this progression is an ongoing conversation between the helper and leader.

INTRODUCTION

On Monday, 13 May 2002, the then secretary of State for Trade & Industry, Patricia Hewitt, gave the Government's response to the report of the Council for Excellence in Management & Leadership. She highlighted a 'lack of leadership within the company and inadequate management', as well as 'bad luck', as the reasons why 37.5% of SMEs close within first three years of operating. But she also could have pointed out a crucial finding by CEML[58] that, when it came to management and leadership provision in SMEs, for many years there has been confusion, starting with central government for over-lapping agendas between various departments, which was partly responsible for a 'jumble of funding drivers'. The result: too much emphasis on the supply of SME learning and development opportunities, without nearly enough attention to stimulation of demand or the factors and circumstances that affect demand.

Many would argue that not a lot has changed since 2002. Certainly, recent changes in Department titles do not seem to have sorted out the over-lapping agendas. However, there has been a change in the talk about SME leadership and development. So, policy and aspiration suggest movement towards a more co-ordinated approach, with a Government *Action Plan for Small Business* seeking to provide a more 'joined-up' service, with a new set of initiatives that seek to stimulate demand and work with informal learning. Thus, a recent programme of management and leadership development, delivered through local Business Links provides 'tailored support and funding for managing directors' in SMEs. More recently, the so-called Leitch Review[59] also highlighted the need to stimulate demand of managers in SMEs for development, although it avoided the crucial area of how this could be achieved.

In this chapter, we will consider more closely the nature of demand by leaders and managers in SMEs for their development. There are two key ideas that the Northern Leadership Academy has worked

---

[58] Perren, L., Davis, M., Kroessin, R. & Hannon, P. (2001). *Mapping of Management & Leadership Development Provisions for SMEs*, London: Council for Excellence in Management & Leadership.

[59] Leitch, S. (2006). *Prosperity for All in the Global Economy – World Class Skills, Final report of the Leitch Review of Skills*, London: HMSO / HM Treasury.

with. First, there is the idea of the SME 'world', which CEML referred to in its findings. This is important because it helped us to think about the lives of managers and leaders, their values and the boundaries they set for what they can and actually do. It is also a reminder that there is not just one type of SME, or one 'world' common to all managers. In a very real sense, each SME manager has his / her own world, which those on the outside must understand if they are have any chance of affecting. Secondly, there is the idea of engagement. In particular, and again making use of the evidence from CEML and others, is the necessity to join the SMEs 'in their world' and to provide support that reflects their personal aspirations and ambitions and enables managers to take ownership of their own development.

LEADERSHIP LEARNING IN SMES

Paradoxically, there is agreement that there is little agreement generally about what leaders do and / or the meaning of leadership. Some even argue that this might be a preferred situation. So, for example, one eminent writer in the field[60] has suggested that 'there's a snowball's chance in hell of redefining leadership in this day and age' and, in the UK, the Government's Performance & Innovation Unit[61] found little agreement on the qualities required for effective leadership and the impact of development programmes on organisational outcomes. Further, many argue that the separation of leadership from management is not particularly helpful and this seems particularly the case in SMEs, where running the business on a day-to-day basis has to be combined with overall responsibility for the ownership, governance and direction of the business. This means that whether it is called 'management' or 'leadership development' is not particularly relevant to SME managers, but what is important is that any learning is closely associated with moving the business in the direction (or not) that reflects the desires and interests of the managers.

---

[60]   Senge, P. (1999). 'The gurus speak (panel discussion): Complexity and organisations', *Emergence* 1(1): 73-91.

[61]   *Strengthening Leadership in the Public Sector*, a study by the Performance & Innovation Unit, published by the Cabinet Office in 2000, www.cabinetoffice.gov.uk.

It is generally agreed, again, that SME managers usually have little time available for anything other than operational activities, so it is hardly surprising that most learning in SMEs of any kind takes place outside a formal education setting. Instead, whether it works or not, SME managers seem to prefer to learn by consulting with people like themselves, customers and suppliers and their staff. Crucially, such consultations are unlikely to be about learning; they will be about working or other features of life. So, even if these interactions do result in the manager learning something, it may not be recognised as learning by the managers themselves, because it is just part of normal working and getting on. There is a massive amount of evidence for the importance of such informal learning in SMEs. This involves doing anything, exploring, experimenting, copying, problem-solving, opportunities taken and lessons from mistakes made in the process. What this means is that learning in SMEs, by leaders and others, is mainly an everyday occurrence and possibly has no ending, so long as the SME survives. Whatever experience people acquire in their everyday life ends up as part of the learning process. Here, the experiences of managers is vital, because what they learn is likely also to feed into the rest of the business, because SME leaders are far more likely to be involved in most aspects of work and changes that are made. They cannot remain on the 'outside', even if that might actually be the best approach sometimes.

The connection between informal learning and SME management and leadership development now is being recognised. For example, the Government's *Action Plan for Small Business* seeks to provide a more 'joined-up' service and a new set of initiatives on a broad front that attempt to stimulate demand and work with informal learning, using brokers to ensure a match between SME needs and provision. The CBI recognises the importance of informal learning by pointing out that, while SMEs may do less formal training, SMEs are more likely to see the skills of their staff as a major factor.[62]

Of course, because of the highly-varied nature of SMEs and their managers, how such managers learn, even from informal events, will also vary. A crucial factor is the disposition of managers towards the growth and performance of the organisation. The evidence

---

[62]   See the CBI's *Informality Works: A New Approach to Training for SMEs*, published in 2003.

consistently shows that many SME managers are more concerned about survival rather than growth. All sorts of factors, internal and external, can influence this concern: for example, industry structure and competition, or education and previous training. For many SMEs, the inherited values from family ownership will impact on learning. We also know that most SMEs seem to lack the desire to plan strategically, and most do not understand their critical success factors. So, the very idea of strategy development and long-term business growth, more often than not, is relegated to the background or do not feature at all in the 'thinking' of SMEs.

There has been strong evidence on performance measurement in SMEs.[63] We know that SME managers rarely have the time for anything other than operational activities and that this stops the move towards more long-term measures of performance. There is also little time available for proper analysis of performance so, even if models are employed, implementation tends to be incomplete or incorrect. Again, informality is emphasised, with little attempt to plan measurement; instead, it is responsive to, and emerges from, solving problems, the consequence of which is that any measures that emerge are reactive towards what has already happened and are developed to bring things under control.

THE DEMAND FOR LEADERSHIP DEVELOPMENT IN SMEs

The various dispositions of SME managers towards learning and such factors suggests a variety of possibilities for establishing demand for management and leadership development. We have found it useful to simplify a little and to summarise the possibilities along an axis, ranging from highly-informal learning to highly-formal learning. **Figure 7.1** represents a scale of possibilities where 1 = highly informal and 5= highly formal.

---

[63]   Garengo, P., Biazzo, S. & Bititci, U.S. (2005). 'Performance measurement systems in SMEs: A review for a research agenda', *International Journal of Management Reviews* 7(1): 25-47.

FIGURE 7.1: THE NATURE OF LEARNING IN SMEs

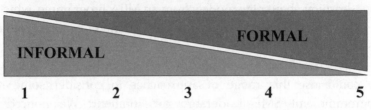

Figure 7.1 suggests five possible approaches to learning and provision. We are reasonably clear about the extremes of highly-informal and highly-formal, but we also need to consider the in-between possibilities of approaches 2, 3 and 4. We began discussions with stakeholders to consider some of the factors that might determine an approach to learning at position 2 (relatively-informal) or position 4 (relatively-formal). We also used the published evidence to develop the meanings. As a result, the following emerged:

- **Place:** It is important to consider where learning takes place, ranging from purely on-site activity to more formal settings, such as class-rooms or offsite training suites. There is a variation in between. For example, a manager might be prepared to move away from where work is actually taking place but still remain on-site. This would explain position 2.

- **Problem:** This considers the degree to which a problem must be solved promptly, with very concrete tools or ideas for immediate application, or whether abstract ideas can be applied more loosely to a range of problems now and in the future. So, learning about problems theoretically on a training programme, but with some prompts on use at work, might explain position 4.

- **Sociality:** The social setting of learning and who is involved in the talk that takes place. This can range from those who are immediately present and part of the problem-solving process to working with experts and others who may not be familiar with a manager. Managers who are prepared to learn with other managers from other organisations would explain position 3.

- **Impact:** This considers how immediately any changes through learning are expected to become apparent. This ranges from immediate application, as and when required, to a view that the impact can be deferred and / or given time to work. Thus learning about new models from an MBA programme, which can be used later in a manager's career, might be considered at position 5.

We could use this range of approaches to consider some recent programmes of SME leadership development. We noticed very quickly that the demand for development was mainly informal, using coaches, mentors, advisers, etc., who work with managers at work, on issues that were immediately meaningful to managers. We could see that this was mainly position 2. It reinforced the evidence from research, emphasising the 'soft' relation-building approaches within SME advising. The more we considered what was happening in the programmes, the more it became clearer that the majority of SME leaders preferred position 2 learning – that is, either one-to-one training relating to a specific skill area or a mentoring / coaching process, usually covering a range of issues. Some managers were also happy to undertake training programmes or to attend conferences (position 4), but we found that informal learning activities, particularly coaching, scored twice as well as training on impact and satisfaction, and better than seminars.

We also found that, given that most managers prefer informal learning, much of what is on offer on the market, in terms of the supply of management and leadership development, is at least one or two levels too high (position 4 rather than position 2). In other words, while much of the provision available for SMEs is similar to the more general leadership and management development for larger organisations, what many SME managers want and gain benefit from is provision that is tailored to their needs specifically, delivered on-site, as close to their work context as possible. Therefore, it is not very surprising that so many initiatives in SME leadership development do not hit the target, especially those managers who avoid initiatives, even if they know about them and could get support to attend.

We have to open the door more carefully on the world of the SME and, we suggest, this needs a stance that allows consideration of current needs, desires and capabilities that are meaningful within a manager's world, the variation in that world and the limits for anything introduced into that world. Anyone who seeks to engage with an SME manager to bring some form of learning to the business needs to understand how to connect with the manager's interests, and to work out what is possible to introduce to the manager and what is not possible. If a success can be achieved, however small, then a journey of learning can begin; the manager can be stretched towards the 'buds' or 'flowers' of development.

SETTING-UP ENGAGEMENT

Engaging with SME managers and leaders to provide development, especially with those who have previously failed to respond to any initiatives, is not an easy process. In our review of the evidence of programmes aimed at SME managers and leaders, we found a small number of consultants or brokers who seemed very skilled at finding 'non-engaged' managers and moving them towards the first stages of development, by getting them to express what they needed and wanted to achieve and summarising this as a Personal Development Plan. In terms of the learning dimension in **Figure 7.1**, non-engaged managers are not considered as non-learning managers; instead, their learning occurs informally through problem-solving and interactions with peers, customers and suppliers. Such learning, even if not recognised as learning, is at position 1 and, for some, this can remain their preference, even if there is a path of growth that can be achieved without outside help – and there is plenty of evidence that some SME managers can mature without external support. However, most do not mature and can become stuck, or even lost, failing to move beyond basic operational activities and limited short-term measures – this is the survival stance of many SME leaders. We have been very interested to understand how engagement could occur with such managers, with the potential for helping managers to grow and develop.

To understand better how engagement with non-engaged managers occurred, we arranged to meet with two consultants / brokers to explore their ways of working. It soon became clear that their work usually involved physically attempting to call on managers in particular locations, so we called such people 'door-knockers'. The method we used to collect data was to ask for short stories of engagement with four managers.

It was clear that engagement was both a strategic and tactical process. The consultants formed a clear plan of engagement, using information from Business Link on target organisations (the non-engaged) and the overall reward package to set targets for achievement. They purchased a database of SMEs, which they cross-checked with Business Link to ensure a match against grant criteria and to avoid duplication with other consultants. This left them with around 500 organisations that they might possibly engage with. For each organisation engaged, payment would be received only if a Personal Development Plan (PDP) was completed, setting out the needs and desires of the managers, the approach to be adopted and the measurement of impact. What was particularly striking was the careful attention given to the formal plan for engagement, with clear targets to be achieved over six months, to ensure commercial viability.

The process of engagement begins with an attempt to attract managers into a conversation. As outsiders, they needed to consider the interests and concerns of those to whom it is directed. It is an unpredictable process in the early stages and relies on the extent to which the outsider can connect to the interests of those being addressed. It soon becomes clear that a failure to make a conversation is also failure to engage. Much of the work to engage requires conversations with others who stand / sit between the target managers and the consultants. A key difficulty was 'getting through receptionists to secretaries'. However, the approach employed was to attract these others into a conversation too. Friday afternoons were used to make phone calls, and sensitivity to how responses were made allowed progress to be made. The guiding principle demonstrates this sensitivity:

> 'It's all about gauging the response of the person on the end of the phone.'

In one case, a receptionist in a 'good mood' allowed a joke to be used and a conversation to be initiated about the programme, which the 'MD would be mad to miss out on'. There was a successful outcome, although not without minor hurdles of four missed return phone calls. Eventually, a connection was made and, sensing again a particular mood and stance, the consultant could reassure the manager that 'it will not take long and I am not going to sit there for half an hour trying to sell you something'. The attraction was the £1,000 grant to meet the needs identified, although such attraction is also affected by previous experiences with grant applications; perceptions of 'heavy paperwork' prove to be a frequently-encountered image. It is not usually a lack of awareness that prevents access to SME initiatives but perceptions of the time involved to begin participation. Thus, the consultant was able to pre-empt potential resistance by reassurance on the possibility 'of wasting the manager's time'. Based on the promise of 'five minutes to tell you all about it', an immediate action to meet was achieved.

The consultant then, on entering the office, seeks to find sufficient indicators that will ensure that a conversation will take place. In one case, he noticed football and golf photos on the wall and an interest in cars. This allowed some 'common ground' to be established 'in plain English'; to reach agreement for a return visit to deal specifically with management and leadership needs in this case required a 15-minute conversation that established the social credentials of the consultant. The result of this was the removal of 'threat'. Key data was gathered quickly to ensure 'eligibility' for the project, to be completed on the required documentation by the consultant, rather than 'wasting the manager's time'. Time between the first and second visit also allows time for consideration of possibilities. Some managers are already clear about needs, but most require help. Even at the second conversation, golf and football provide the means to move into a more focused discussion of needs. The formality of the Training Needs Analysis and the artefact of a form are downplayed, to ensure the conversation does not turn against the established flow. Only at a suitable conclusion, when needs are clear and agreed, does the 'what we need to do for Business Link' utterance occur. So, common ground (we both like golf and football) leads 'a relationship of trust' and the consultant can now align his interests with the manager's to become a *we* against Business Link.

However, the consultant also must remain in common interest with Business Link, which requires correct completion of documentation, in return for which the consultant earns his fee. As an 'intermediary', the consultant works between the worlds of the quasi-public agency and that of the SME. All the forms are completed by the consultant in his office, and returned by e-mail to the manager for confirmation. Once achieved, the conversation is hardened into a PDP, officially recognised as the start of engagement with the manager – he 'is in control' and can spend up to £1,000 on his own development.

The help initiated by the consultant may require others to form a relationship with the manager. In one case, this was a training provider who could meet the needs of the manager. The danger here, of course, is that the training provider does not yet know the SME manager and could be prone to generalisations rather than close understanding. The work completed so far is now at risk, so the consultant attempts to reduce the risk by being present at the first meeting ensuring that the 'chemistry is right'.

The importance of such a presence is evident in another case, where the process of contact by telephone quickly leads to a visit. The consultant avoids the 'the big conversation on the phone' and moves quickly towards 'let me come and see you', which is regarded as fundamental in building the relationship. Interestingly, through Business Link and their marketing agents, several thousand flyers had been sent to SMEs, although this seldom resulted in engagement. On arrival at the office of Case B, the consultant seeks the indicators that reflect his own interest and provide the basis for a conversation opening. This needs to be something 'real' rather than imaginary; the consultant does not claim an ability to 'wing it'. He notices many signed football shirts with links to the past – England 1966 and Pele – and guitars signed by U2 and Eric Clapton. Using the latter to set the tune(!), 'the ice was quickly broken' leading to a 90-minute conversation, including a widening of the context to include family – the engagement process was leading towards friendship, too.

A second visit occurs two weeks later, to discuss 'spending your money'. The first 20 minutes ensures re-engagement on the basis of previous understanding – they discuss the purchase of new signed football shirts. This conversational space now can encompass desires and needs for management and leadership. The consultant assesses the potential for learning and the limits; it is a process of mutual problem-solving, seeking opportunities for learning that will have tangible benefits for the manager and his business. For the manager, the questions test the various options, leading to a clear formulation of desires. For the consultant, there is a widening of his network, not only a new 'friend' but also the seeking of another source of expertise to bring into the relationship, who has the 'right chemistry'. He has to ensure that, at each stage, there is an understanding based on a 'common subject'; there has to be enough shared perspective to achieve common understanding.

In another case, engagement seemed more straightforward, at first. The initial phone conversation appeared to indicate virtual engagement was possible and a willingness by the manager to complete forms online. However, these were not returned, so the consultant sought once again to present himself at the organisation. The consultant has learnt that 'you cannot rely on people to print things off, you've really got to hold their hands, if necessary'. The danger of virtual engagement is a lack of understanding of the SME world and, only by being 'present', can the sensibilities of managers be 'gauged' to avoid 'patronisation'. Paradoxically, the consultant quickly sensed that he needed to take 'control' ,if engagement was to 'get off the ground'. The simple act of arriving to engage with the manager gave direction to the process and ensured a new meeting was arranged. At the second meeting with two managers from the business, questioning over an hour allowed a widening of scope that revealed the focus of concern, the issue for provision, and the preferences for learning, which together formed the 'comfort zone' for learning. There was an aversion to purely theoretical learning and off-site delivery resulted in a marketing mentor becoming part of the relationship. Again, 'chemistry' was considered the vital marker for transition and the consultant ensures achievement through the 'presence' of all parties.

In a final case, again it appeared straightforward initially. A phone call, direct contact with the manager and a quick appointment suggested that progress to a PDP would be smooth. Even the effects of a 'ram-raid' at the business could not prevent this and became the initial topic of conversation. However, after agreeing to a second appointment to produce the PDP, the manager failed to return calls and the consultant suspected that engagement could not occur. An alternative approach was discovered by chance, while working with another manager, where the manager revealed his friendship with the manager, 'they were mates'. The consultant sensed he could use this connection to 'piggy-back' towards re-engagement with the manager :

'Can you tell Daniel, the next time you speak to him, that I am after him?'. Soon after, contact was made and the friendship between the two managers provided a new angle for the conversation that the consultant could employ through story-telling at his meeting.

SUMMARY

In the UK, 99% of firms are considered to be small businesses / SMEs; they employ 12.6 million people. Such organisations are considered essential to improving productivity and as a source of innovation. However, many of these organisations become stuck in a fight for survival with short-term measures of 'success', learning mainly by reacting to everyday problems. Leadership is severely limited in such circumstances, assuming that most owner-managers have some aspiration to move beyond the survival world. That we need to consider the SME 'world' as the starting point for learning is now recognised by policy-makers, with a trend towards the provision of demand-led support using informal learning. Evidence from various programmes and research suggests to us that there is a pattern emerging, which confirms that informal learning is preferred by SME managers, whatever the issue considered This further suggests that we need to consider how to engage with SME managers at the right time, the right level of learning and the right consideration of their interests.

If this pattern is confirmed from around the country, and research suggests this is likely, then we need to consider how to provide support in terms of informal relationships that work softly on building relationships with SMEs. We need approaches that understand the uniqueness of SME worlds and, how through talk and dialogue, SME managers can be engaged with to consider their learning and the development of their organisations. We have seen the value of this in the work of the consultants / brokers considered above. The offering of money was not enough in terms of attraction; it required a lot of effort and persistence, sometimes indirectly, to achieve a 'presence' with managers and then considerable skills of conversation, drawing on stories, jokes, chit-chat and anything else to hand, to ensure engagement actually happens that could be completed, resulting in an agreement for development. Establishing demand for leadership and management development in SMEs means that we need to find more 'door-knockers'.

8

MATCHING DEMAND TO PROVISION IN SMEs

This chapter provides a framework for matching SME managers and leaders with appropriate provision.

We base our evidence on research relating to SME learning, in particular the strong emphasis that is given in the literature to informal learning and the types of provision available. This research acknowledges that significant learning takes place, as a consequence of working on work-related problems.

Although this learning can be characterised as occurring 'naturally', if 'problems' or 'opportunities' can be structured and knowledge fed in, in a flexible way, learning can be enhanced.

INTRODUCTION

In the United Kingdom, various Government-backed initiatives have sought to promote learning and development in small and medium-sized enterprises (SMEs). However, the SME response to such initiatives remains mixed, to say the least, and there remains an apparent lack of consistency and co-ordination. For management and leadership provision, there has been particular confusion, with central government responsible for over-lapping agendas between Departments and a 'jumble of funding drivers'[64] leading to an over-emphasis on the supply of SME learning and development opportunities, without sufficient attention to the stimulation of demand. As has long been argued, bureaucrats and others who design SME training should not enforce their structure on small firms but rather should look towards the way that SMEs learn and work. In the last chapter, we pointed to the recognition that it is informal learning that should be given prominence in SME management and leadership development and that this should underpin a shift to demand-led interventions. Evidence of the recognition of the need for a demand-led informal learning approach can be seen in the UK Government's *Action Plan for Small Business*, which seeks to provide a more 'joined-up' service and a set of initiatives on a broad front that attempt to stimulate demand and work with informal learning, using brokers to ensure a match between SME needs and provision.

In this chapter, we focus on how such a match can be understood and achieved, by presenting a map of leadership and management development possibilities available for SMEs. The map considers the two key features of learning and provision:

- The various dispositions of SME managers towards learning, ranging from highly-informal to formal.

- The form of provision, which must respond to needs, ranging from highly-operational to strategic.

The result is a map that reflects the various 'worlds' of SME managers and posits 25 domains of SME management and leadership

---

[64]   Perren, L., Davis, M. & Kroessin, R. (2001). *Mapping of Management & Leadership Development Provisions for SMEs*, London: Council for Excellence in Management & Leadership.

possibilities. Using data from our consideration of evidence, we can suggest the pattern of provision against the need for it. We then can suggest some of the possibilities for provision – in particular, the methods of development that seem to work. Finally, we suggest a developmental ladder that can be used to provide direction to policy and interventions efforts.

THE DEMAND & SUPPLY OF LEARNING IN SMES

In **Chapter 7,** *Establishing Demand,* we suggested that most learning in SMEs takes place outside a formal education setting, with SME managers learning significantly from peers, customers and suppliers, by doing, exploring, experimenting, copying, problem-solving, with opportunities taken and lessons learnt from mistakes made in the process. Learning in SMEs is mainly an everyday phenomenon and possibly has no ending. Therefore, whatever experience people acquire in their everyday life ends up as part of the learning process.

When CEML[65] calls for collaborated efforts to join SMEs in their world, by providing support that reflects their personal aspirations and ambitions and enables managers to take ownership of their own development, this immediately raises issues concerning how their 'world' is understood, the terms of such understanding and whether this reflects the meanings of SME managers?

In the previous chapter, we represented the variety of possibilities for establishing demand for management and leadership development in SMEs as a dimension ranging from highly-informal learning, where preference is given to learning at work on issues relating to solving real problems, to highly-formal by attending events, usually away from the workplace, that are designed for learning, including the recognition of outcomes through accreditation. Other occasions represent a mixture of informal and formal, to a greater or lesser extent. We have represented this dimension of learning possibilities earlier in **Figure 7.1** (see p.88).

---

[65]   CEML (2002). *Joining Entrepreneurs in their World,* London: Council for Excellence in Management & Leadership.

We also used the published evidence and discussion with stakeholders to develop the meanings of different positions along the dimension. This identified the importance of factors, such as where learning takes place, the degree to which a problem must be solved promptly, the social setting of learning and how immediate any changes through learning are expected to become apparent.

In addition to the SME managers' disposition towards learning, we also need to consider what is provided to them. One of CEML's crucial findings with respect to the provision of management and leadership development for SMEs was the plethora of publicly-funded schemes, often perceived to be overly-bureaucratic and disconnected from the needs of SMEs but driven by Government agendas and funding. As a consequence, there is little take-up of such schemes among SMEs, although there can be a relatively high awareness and understanding of the initiatives, despite low usage. One of the dangers of the supply-side mentality has been the simplistic assumptions about SME life, which usually results in scaled-down versions of management and leadership skills derived from what large organisations do.

Also, it is argued that SME managers generally are more disposed towards short-term planning and do not seek to expand their operations like large enterprises. Research into SMEs in the UK and other European countries indicate that many SMEs only aspire to survival and independence, rather than to substantial business growth. A significant influence on appropriate provision of management and leadership development is the connection to performance measurement. A recent systematic review of literature[66] in this field suggested five characteristics of SMEs and performance:

- SMEs find it difficult to participate in performance measurement projects because of the lack of time available for anything other than operational activities.

- Even where a performance model is employed, the implementation tends to be partial or incorrect – a consequence perhaps of most models being more suited to larger organisations.

---

[66]   Garengo, P., Biazzo, S. & Bititci, U.S. (2005). 'Performance measurement systems in SMEs: A review for a research agenda', *International Journal of Management Reviews* 7(1): 25-47.

- Performance measurement is narrowly-focused, usually on financial and operational aspects, with little awareness for integration or systemic consideration.

- Performance measurement is not planned but is responsive to, and emerges, from solving problems, the consequence of which is that any measures that emerge are past-oriented and developed to support control.

- There is little resource available for formal data analysis, and the preference for informality often results in ambiguous measures and objectives.

Various internal and external factors have been identified as taking a toll on SME success / growth. These factors include industry structure and competition, decisions, employee relations, objectives, organisational culture, education and training, and prior experience. Growth in the SME sector is mostly seen from the angle of capital growth and / or employment generation, which can be seen as inappropriate, and misplaced. Others argue that although SMEs are 'tiny drops of water that make the mighty ocean', and have the potential to grow, the situation on the ground is that many SMEs wish to remain 'tiny', and that SMEs lack the desire to plan strategically, not to mention the lack of understanding by SMEs of their critical success factors. Strategy development and long-term business growth, more often than not, are relegated to the background or do not feature at all in the 'thinking' of SMEs.[67]

The dispositions of SME managers toward performance measurement and growth manifest themselves in their response to the provision of management and leadership skills. For many SMEs, survival and the constraint of current operations are the priority. Managers are pre-occupied with meeting short-term goals and use measurement processes accordingly. As a consequence, the management and leadership skills required are those that help fulfil such operations. By contrast, there are some managers who are able to move towards long-term planning, using more systemic approaches to performance measurement and seek more strategic learning. We

---

[67] HM Treasury (2003). *Enterprise Britain: A Modern Approach to Meeting the Enterprise Challenge*, Norwich: HMSO.

present this polarisation as a dimension of possible provision of management and leadership development, shown in **Figure 8.1**.

FIGURE 8.1: POSSIBLE PROVISION OF MANAGEMENT & LEADERSHIP DEVELOPMENT

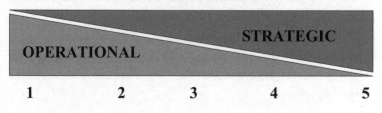

We also developed criteria for assessing management and leadership development provision:

- **Time-frame:** A key feature of provision is the length of time needed for it to impact on the manager and / or organisation. At position 1, the expectation is for immediate impact, while the expectation at position 5 is five years or more.

- **Horizon:** This considers how provision broadens the scope of thinking of managers. It ranges from the short-term, and satisfaction with the *status quo*, to long-term and thinking 'outside the box' or radical thinking. This is a crucial factor for managers and needs to consider the extent to which a manager's understanding can be 'stretched'.

- **Measurement:** Any provision implies how performance is measured. This could range from immediate task performance, to targets against performance, to more systemic approaches to measurement.

- **Ownership:** This considers the process of any provision and how it occurs. Ownership ranges from self at position 1, to involved others at position 2, to outside experts at position 5

- **Cost:** Participating in any learning activity requires some cost, whether it is in terms of time, commitment and / or money.

These two dimensions of learning and provision can be combined to provide a framework for matching the requirements of SME managers for development with possible provision. This framework is shown as **Figure 8.2**.

FIGURE 8.2: A FRAMEWORK FOR MATCHING THE DEVELOPMENT REQUIREMENTS OF SME MANAGERS WITH PROVISION

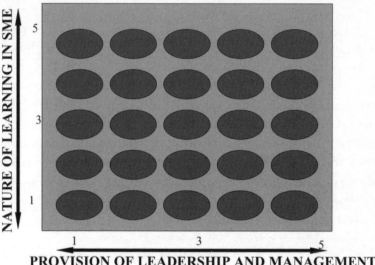

This framework suggests 25 possible combinations of learning and provision. The value of this framework, based on key factors relating to the nature of learning and provision for SME management and leadership development, is its use in helping to understand learning preferences of SME managers and their desires and expectations for any provision – this is the SME 'world'.

Each combination represents a possible position based on particular judgements about learning (L) and provision (P) – for example, L1P1 indicates a learning preference that is highly-informal and provision that needs to be highly-operational. We suggest that this is *normal* working for many SMEs, based on survival, where learning is highly-instrumental, concerned with solving problems in the here and now, with little or no intervention from others apart from those who are part of the immediate situation. From this position, some SME managers can make progress without externally-funded business support, perhaps progressing from L1P1 to L1P2, L1P3 and beyond. That is, they continue to learn informally, but are able to stretch the provision required by obtaining resources from their own activities. We might call such organisations 'pure entrepreneurial'.

More typically, managers in such a position are those who fail to respond to help from external providers and Government- or European Union-funded initiatives – these are the 'hard to reach' or 'tough nuts to crack'. Engaging with SME managers and leaders in this position to provide development, especially with those who have previously failed to respond to any initiatives, is not an easy process. Many such SMEs may not aspire to grow; others do but are foiled by current necessities; and others may aspire to grow but are stuck with traditional but less cost-effective work methods that lead towards decline and eventual closure. Stimulating demand for management, leadership and business development among such SMEs requires more understanding of the nature of SMEs – their 'world' – and how resources can be more carefully-focused.

PROVISION THAT WORKS

There is growing evidence on working with managers in a local context setting, on issues that are meaningful to them using coaches, mentors, advisers – often referred to as 'intermediaries', who can give importance to 'soft' relation-building approaches, which can stimulate demand that is mainly informal. As we showed in **Chapter 7,** ***Establishing Demand in SMEs***, recent research on a group of intermediaries who specialise in engagement with SME managers and leaders suggests the importance of persistent efforts to create the conditions for a conversation that can eventually lead to the formation of a plan for learning. Such 'door-knockers' demonstrated considerable skills of conversation, drawing on many examples of stories, jokes, chit-chat and anything else to hand, to ensure a path to engagement.

This practice is at the heart of the matching process, although it is certainly an expensive option, requiring one-to-one attention. If we consider the SME world as the starting point for learning, evidence from various programmes and research suggests an emerging pattern that confirms, first, that informal learning is preferred by SME managers and, second, that, with engagement with SME managers at the right time, the right level of learning and the right consideration of their interests, a match with appropriate provision can be found.

Indeed, one of the most exciting developments has been how SME managers can be moved to consider new possibilities beyond their current capabilities for themselves and their organisations. For example, if L1 is learning without external assistance, all levels beyond L1 imply assistance. It becomes important for those engaging and assisting to understand just what those current capabilities are, not just in standard terms, but in terms meaningful within the manager's world, which are bound to be subject to all sorts of variation. If engagers and advisers can explore the SME world, composed of managers' present interests, desires, concerns and core capabilities, they can also consider how far provision, for whatever is deemed appropriate, can stretch the manager. We represent the situation diagrammatically in **Figure 8.3**.

FIGURE 8.3: STRETCHING SME MANAGERS & LEADERS

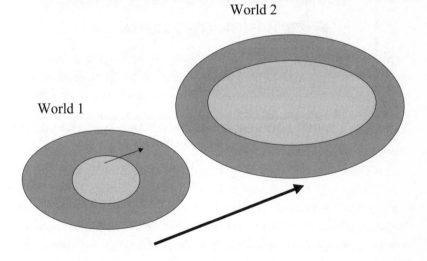

Current capabilities are shown as the inner oval in World 1. Interventions, if access is granted, can work with the capabilities and then move into the area between the inner oval and the outer boundary. Movement beyond the boundary would not be in the interests of the manager. However, over time, it may be possible that the command of new capabilities from support make it appropriate to move into a new world, World 2, where the process can start again. There is also an implication of the development of a relationship with an adviser who understands the dynamics of such a process. Part of this understanding also could be to appreciate a manager's current position on the framework and future moves to new positions, as shown in **Figure 8.4**.

FIGURE 8.4: CURRENT & FUTURE WORLDS FOR SME MANAGERS

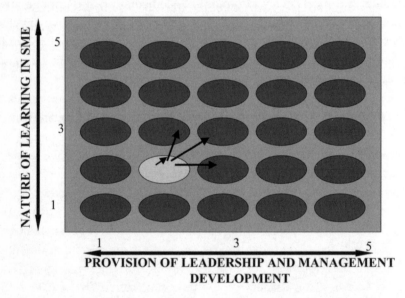

It becomes evident that, starting from L1P1, engagement that leads to valued provision eventually can mean that sufficient stretch is allowed, moving to L2P2. Learning becomes relatively more formal, probably through a mentor or coach, and focuses on provision that meets requirements beyond day-to-day problem-solving.

However, from this position, over time, more possibilities can be offered. For example, there could be an opportunity to work one-to-one with a mentor. We have evidence that this is quite possible, with some significant stretch being possible (see for example, **Case Example 1** at the end of this chapter). This keeps the learning at L2, but the manager is introduced to increasingly more strategic provision, at a pace that is in tune with his / her requirements.

Other possibilities include a move to L3P2 or P3, where learning also can embrace sharing problems with other managers. We know that SME managers often are prepared to discuss their concerns with other managers who can relate to their interests. There already exist a number of local networks and forums that provide a context for this process. For example, the Yorkshire Leadership Group runs a programme of facilitated peer group development, with participants from a wide range of non-competing organisations. Each group has no more than 15 members and meets every two months. Members can also arrange one-to-one business coaching, mentoring, advisory or non-executive director services to supplement the group meetings. Managers may not regard it as learning, but there is a possibility that changes in behaviour and organisation performance can occur as a consequence.

A step up from informal networks are programmes that seek to create similar conditions of peer informality and challenge, but put learning more centrally into the process. For example, we have recent evidence from the evaluation of a regional Action Learning for Leaders programme for SMEs for over 150 SME managers, which suggested significant benefits where the chance to reflect on and question key issues within a context of challenge and support led to actions to overcome constraints faced. Action learning has also been shown to be successful in programmes supported by the Sector Skills Councils in addressing leadership development for micro and SME owner-managers. The Action Learning for Leaders programme ran from 2004 to 2006, with three groups of SME owner-managers in Glasgow, Nottingham and Guildford. The results were rigorously evaluated. The process of Action Learning and on-the-job coaching proved to be very successful. Some of the comments from the participants included:

'I have benefited greatly from this programme and have been able to bring the benefits directly back to my business.'

'The programme has really helped me to gain the confidence and achieve changes.'

'This programme has probably saved my company from potential oblivion on my retirement.'

Working in collaboration with the Northern Leadership Academy, a number of action learning sets have been established, including, in Sheffield, a learning set programme called 'Six-Squared', designed to enable peer-to-peer learning. In addition, after nine months of participation, there is an option for Six-Squared members to begin their own action learning set using the basic principles of action learning. This creates the potential to multiply the number of participants involved into several hundred over time. As reported, 'the model is designed to be a sustainable "self-help" approach, which is entrepreneur-led and does not depend on external agencies or government funding'.[68] There are also action learning sets operating in Leeds, Manchester, Liverpool, Huddersfield and Bradford.

It also has become apparent that the move to more formality, and the chance to escape operational concerns for some, has been a key feature in becoming more strategic and more capable as leaders. Recent research suggests that SME managers and leaders need space to think strategically, so that new ideas can be considered and absorbed into normal work.[69] Such spaces or 'strategic space' has been in evidence in programmes that also encourage peer learning, combined with coaching and mentoring. This moves managers into positions such as L4P3 and beyond on the framework. For example, the pilots of the LEAD programme at Lancaster University between November 2005 and March 2006 incorporated coaching, mentoring and peer learning, as well as strategic workshops led by experts. The evaluation revealed the importance of the 'soft aspects' of formal provision, including the acknowledgement of the need for affirmation and growth in confidence, principally achieved by building relationships, supported by reflective and peer learning. Similarly, the consultancy Leading Your People to Success recently completed a project working with 24 SME companies simultaneously. Entitled PIP (People, Innovation & Productivity), it

---

[68] Taken from the interim evaluation of the *Six-Squared Learning Sets for Entrepreneurs & Small Business Owners,* Sheffield University, December 2007.

[69] Thorpe, R., Holt, R., Macpherson, A. & Pittaway, L. (2007). *Studying the Evolution of Knowledge within Small & Medium-sized Firms,* London: Economic & Social Research Council / Engineering & Physical Sciences Research Council.

served to improve their cultures. Each company received a bespoke approach, based on findings from an initial benchmark.

A second survey, approximately 12 months later, concluded:

- £4.9 million (8.8%) increase in Gross Value Added.

- 44.7% increase in profit.

- Increase in productivity / employee of £1,176 (4.3%).

These are exciting developments and potentially provide an opportunity to advance SME learning on a large scale. **Figure 8.5** shows possible growth paths for SME management and leadership development.

FIGURE 8.5: SME GROWTH PATHS

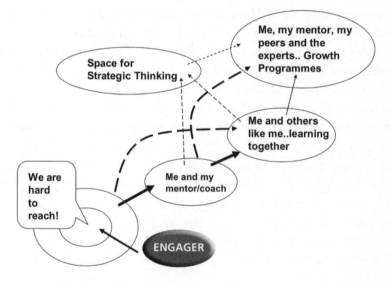

SUMMARY

This chapter provides a framework for matching SME managers and leaders with appropriate provision. It is based on evidence and research relating to SME learning, in particular the strong emphasis given in such literature to informal learning, and the types of provision available. We have sought to show answers to questions such as:

- How do we get SMEs to embrace, and avail themselves of, provisions in their world?

- How do we ensure that there are coherent provisions that will ensure clarity of where SMEs are and provide for progress without missing out on their actual needs?

- How can we engage SMEs to 'stretch' their thinking beyond what they have now to where, how, when, who, which ways of doing things better for future purposes?

CASE EXAMPLE 1

LEADERSHIP IN SMEs

'TRAINING, IT'S A LOAD OF B*****KS':
THE STORY OF THE HAIRDRESSER & HIS 'SUIT'

Mark Riley, whose words appear in the title of this case study, is a well-known hairdresser in Huddersfield[70] but, for many years, his views about learning and development were typical of many SME managers. More concerned about survival than growth, he had a poor, even antagonistic, record in responding to training initiatives and was highly sceptical of the benefits of such initiatives. Nevertheless, by the end of this story something rather wonderful happens.

Mark may have been 'stuck and struggling' in running his business, and this may have been the pattern for 19 years but, in the last two years, things have changed, starting with attraction into a programme for his own development and engagement with a mentor, his 'Suit', and moving on to develop staff and to set up a training academy to provide skills for his version of how hairdressing can provide just what his customers want. It is a story that shows just how 'a goldmine' can be exploited, based on the learning and development of the manager, which allows the business to grow, and which in turn provides for further learning and development of staff and trainees. Therefore, the story carries some key messages for everyone concerned with helping small businesses to grow and their owners to develop as leaders.

It was through a 'door-knocker', Kent Mayall of Inspire to Independence,[71] that Mark became aware of how he could 'exploit his goldmine'. But this awareness was not achieved without a struggle. First, it took five telephone calls before Mark agreed to meet Kent and

---

70   You can contact Mark Riley at mark@mark-riley.co.uk.

71   You can contact Kent at kent.mayall@i2i-ltd.co.uk.

then it took a further four meetings before Mark's scepticism subsided and he agreed to meet Brian Wadsworth,[72] a specialist mentor of SME managers, over 'breakfast in a café'. Importantly, through this series of meetings, Mark's needs and desires became more evident and he ended up no longer 'stuck and struggling', but now a 'man with a plan for change', which he agreed to implement with Brian.

Working with Brian, Mark soon identified 'major inefficiencies' in current operations that were causing cash-flow problems; indeed, the business was a 'mess'. One change needed was a supervisory infrastructure that would allow Mark more time to focus on operational and financial performance. He could also take time away from 'cutting hair' to meet with Brian to think strategically and to talk business. Part of this talk was to articulate Mark's special vision of the 'Mark Riley Experience', based on a 'journey of well-being for customers' and growth of the business to over 10 salons across Yorkshire by 2010.

This vision also would need trained staff who could enact the values that went with the vision. So it was not enough that trainees went college to get their NVQ in Hairdressing; it was also important that trainees understood and worked with Mark's notion of the 'journey' and the experience of 'well-being' by the customers. One way to ensure this was to do more training in-house, rather than at the college. So, with Brian's help, a partnership deal was struck with Brighouse College to allow Mark to establish an academy for 20 trainees, with a forecast to expand to 50 as the business grows. As a result, Mark can select trainees against his criteria of quality that reflect his aspirations for growth.

There are some crucial lessons to consider from this story:[73]

- First, as a 'hard-to-reach' SME ,who nevertheless had long-frustrated aspirations for growth and development, Mark required a real person, and persistent efforts by that person, to secure engagement into a process of development. Like many SME managers, Mark did not lack awareness of support, but his

---

[72]　You can contact Brian at brian@isds2.co.uk.

[73]　For a full account of this case, see Gold, J. ,Thorpe, R., Riley, M., Mayall, K. & Wadsworth, B. (2007). *"Training, It's a Load of B*****ks": The Story of the Hairdresser & His Suit*, HRD Annual Conference, Oxford Brookes University, Oxford.

experience of such offerings failed to attract him. And yet, for nearly 20 years, Mark had suspected that his business also was a 'goldmine, waiting for exploitation'. Furthermore, it was not in the classic high-growth sector that this opportunity was possible but, based on his vision and aspiration, Mark was a 'three-legged gazelle', requiring only support for take-off.

- Second, once support had been agreed, coaching and mentoring could be provided to work in tune with Mark's capabilities, interests and desires, but also to stretch Mark into uncharted waters. Once again, this future could be talked about only with someone who understood Mark, but this very process also created the space for conversations to become more strategic.

- Third, at the start of the process of engagement, Mark could access £1,000 to provide for his own development as a manager and leader. Within three months, he was prepared to continue to pay for this development from his own funds. Crucially, he could measure the value he was obtaining from his work with Brian. Indeed, from an initial position of little understanding of any kind of measurement of business performance, through his work with Brian, he had been introduced to and used a range of different measures, including the impact of training on the business. This was part of a more general stretch in strategic understanding that was now possible. In future, public funding for SME development needs to consider carefully how values and measurement are included in the development process.

- Finally, and crucially, business development was the rationale for Mark's management and leadership development and the subsequent training initiatives for his staff. Like many employers, he was not impressed with formal qualifications. Instead, as a passionate believer in his industry, he wanted 'to give something back' and the construction of a future story for his business that provided the backdrop against which skills development could be referenced. This is in contrast to Government policy that suggests skills development from the outside to support business development on the inside. There does need to be more serious attention to the desires and aspirations of SME managers, which can only be accessed from the inside.

CASE EXAMPLE 2

RELEVANT & TIMELY LEARNING FOR BUSY LEADERS

This account of practice reports on an 'action learning set' Leaders Learning Together. Leaders from the retail and leisure sectors were recruited by the Sector Skills Councils, under the sponsorship of the Northern Leadership Academy. At the time of this report, the 'set' had met for eight out of 10 planned sessions. None of the participants had had any previous experience of 'action learning' or 'collaborative learning'. In describing to the group what 'action learning' was, the terms 'peer-to-peer coaching' and 'collaborative learning' were used. This also gave individuals an idea of the processes involved. At the seventh meeting, individuals were asked how they would describe the reality of how the group was functioning and the term 'peer-to-peer coaching' was the most popular description.

Two processes were emphasised within this 'peer-to-peer coaching':

- An 'action-learn-action' process – of bringing along an issue that required action, learning from it and deciding on future action based on the learning.
- A 'support-challenge-support' emphasis – using challenging questioning and supportive listening.

The group was reminded of these processes at every meeting, and it was a particular strength of this group that individuals could transfer skills from other work contexts into the group. A number of leadership issues of importance to this group emerged through the various interactions that took place.

LEADERSHIP ISSUE 1:
BRANDING THE GOLF PROFESSIONAL

One of the issues discussed at the 'learning set' was the branding of Gary, a golf professional. Gary is a successful golfing professional, with a retail outlet on a golf course, a golf training programme, a new website business (400,000 hits a week) and a comprehensive weekly newsletter sent to an audience of 400. One of the issues he wanted to explore was his 'brand', how he could articulate it and then how he could train his staff to emulate it. Gary knew what his brand was, but found it hard to describe it in words.

Through getting to know him, the group were able to help him to translate his feelings into something more concrete, with key messages that he could work on. From the general notion of wanting to be 'well-respected and well-regarded as an expert', the group helped Gary to articulate the key messages of: 'trust, me I deliver'; 'I'll be there for you when you need assistance'; 'I give the "right' advice"'; 'I'm a pro – a golfer through and through – top brass'; 'I am friendly, approachable, available and have time to talk'; 'I have authenticity and genuinely want to help you meet your aspirations'; and 'with me, you can be the élite – the best'.

Having articulated his brand, Gary shared his frustrations that, despite much effort, he couldn't get his staff to emulate his brand in their own behaviour. They were not welcoming people into the shop, or asking them about their game, as he would do. They were not available and approachable to visitors as he was. When someone walked into his shop, they would put their heads down and ignore them. He was really frustrated by this. The group helped Gary to explore how his brand was linked to his personality and that it didn't necessarily link with the staff's. Whereas he was 'natural', they might need specific direction, and even scripts, to help them to emulate what Gary would do naturally. His confidence came from his personality and skills – theirs needed to come from something else – perhaps training. We challenged him to write down exactly the sort of phrases he would use in his communication to customers.

He found this a little odd but, once we had coaxed out a variety of statements, the group showed how he could offer these to his staff as 'ways in' to a conversation when perhaps they just lacked confidence. It was a different perspective for him to consider.

LEADERSHIP ISSUE 2:
DEVELOPING LEADERSHIP IN OTHERS

Another issue brought to the group was how to develop leadership skills in someone who was clearly able to develop into a leader but didn't seem to be progressing. One of the members wanted to put forward one of their staff for leadership training but the person's behaviour was making her question her own judgement. The situation was that, when the leader would feedback to the learner where improvements needed to be made, the learner would agree, confirm she understood, articulate that she understood but then would do nothing to change the behaviour. When we probed a bit more, it became clear that one thing the member found odd was that, despite seeing this person every day, this person would communicate to her through writing – for example, 'thanking her for her time' and 'thanking her for her feedback' – rather than responding face-to-face.

This led to a discussion around assumptions about how people learn and, using Kolb's model, it was felt that the learner was a theoretical learner who preferred written communication and that the improvements needed in her performance needed to be articulated in a more theoretical manner before she could really grasp them. It seemed too simple to be the answer but, using this insight, the leader changed her approach and the results were amazing.

Now the issue was how to help this developing leader to lead other people in other ways than just the theoretical and, in particular, through verbal communication. Activities and exercises were created to provide opportunities for the learner to develop these skills, and confidence in using them, and the report back was that this was working well.

LEADERSHIP ISSUE 3:
CULTURAL ASSUMPTIONS

One of the most powerful aspects of collaborative learning is the way it challenges assumptions that we hold without knowing we do. Another example where collaborative learning helped, and assumptions were challenged, was where there was a recruitment difficulty for a particular post. The IT manager of the hotel run by one of the group members had walked out when a virus had attacked the computer system and he had not managed to fix it. He was clearly capable of doing so from an IT perspective but needed to liaise differently with the IT group headquarters, as this seemed to be the difficulty. The job of IT manager also involved helping guests to log onto the computers in their rooms, which was not a skilled IT task but took up a lot of time. The hotel needed a replacement and had felt the staff they were getting were not right for the role.

When the issue was explored further, it was found that this IT manager was the fifth person to walk out on the job. More exploration was clearly needed. It was stated in passing that the person was required to be on call 24 hours a day, and some members of the learning group felt that this was unusual. However, the hoteliers in the group explained that this was normal practice in the hotel trade. However, the non-hoteliers felt this was not normal in other trades, and in particular in IT, where hours were often 8.30am to 4.30pm. This opened up the discussion and unearthed assumptions that may have been made – that an IT person could adapt to the hotel culture.

The member of the group, in trying to fill-in for his absent IT manager, had spent some time in his IT manager's office and it said it was a 'lonely' place, where he felt quite isolated. As he gave further information, the members of the group 'picked up' on particular aspects, such as the mixture of high-skill and low-skill in the job, the comparatively low pay of the hotel trade compared to the IT trade generally, the possible isolation of the role, and the requirement to be available 24/7 and they questioned assumptions about culture. Here was someone coming from an IT culture into a hotel culture, where things worked very differently. This was a 'light bulb' moment as to what the 'real' problem might be. This was further explored and alternatives became apparent.

The member of the group who employed the IT manager decided to employ an IT agency for the IT part of the job and to train up a computer keen porter (who often helped customers get logged on) to take on the other aspects of the job. Reporting back later, the member indicated that this not only solved the immediate problems but had provided a porter with a new role and had provided a long-term strategy for other hotels to follow.

SUMMARY

This action learning group showed that leaders always will be busy and will have a high sense of responsibility to their businesses and, in particular, to their staff. They want to learn, but see it as a luxury for themselves that sometimes has to be sacrificed. If the learning is timely and relevant, this improves the likelihood of engagement.

9

APPROACHING THE PUBLIC SECTOR: CO-PRODUCTION MODELS

I n this chapter, we identify a range of principles aimed at encouraging and developing effective leadership practice in public sector organisations.

As with those for SMEs, these principles also are based on extensive research and draw upon the experiences and practice of current managers and leaders in public sector organisations.

The model for the development of public sector managers also is problem-centred and learner-centred, recognising the realities and challenges they face. 'Expert' outside assistance serves to facilitate, and the relationship is one of 'in partnership with' rather than expert 'on top of'.

The chapter offers 16 principles of development good practice.

INTRODUCTION

In the Northern Leadership Academy, we have been investigating what is known about the leadership programmes / interventions that work in support of distributed leadership in the public sector (leadership across a public sector organisation).

There is little evidence, but a lot of supposition, in the public sector about:

- What sort of leadership is needed?
- What sorts of development interventions develop these leaders?

Currently, in the public sector, the answer to these questions is usually 'getting the right person at the top'. The answer is always an individual. The principles we have been developing at the NLA demonstrate a different view: that leadership is a collective activity.

In the absence of clear research evidence, we designed a process to access the wisdom of current leaders, working from their experience in the current public sector context, particularly in exploring adaptive leadership. We invited chief executives to join us for a day at a Leadership Summit, bringing with them leaders from their organisations. We spent the day working from these leaders' experiences (their tacit knowledge), both as participants in leadership development interventions, and as purchasers of leadership development, to find out the types of intervention that best enable learning and change which benefits the organisation.

Using the principles

The principles we have developed, and which we explain below, come from an appreciation of 'what works'. We asked current leaders in the public sector to describe their experiences of leadership development where there was a clear, beneficial, organisational impact. We were looking for examples where leadership development led to effective organisational change. By telling stories of experiences, we could access the reality of what happened. We moved from what is 'supposed to work' to what actually works. These principles come from real experiences.

We offer these principles as a starting point for both providers of leadership interventions and for readers seeking to commission leadership development work in your organisation.

A note on language

We use the term 'leadership development intervention' rather than 'leadership development programme' as the Leadership Summit and our own background work demonstrated the need for a range of leadership development activities, not just leadership programmes. 'Programmes' usually conjures up ideas of workshops, classrooms, off-site sessions, time-outs and personal development diagnostics. 'Interventions' offers more of a spectrum, from individual development to organisational development – giving more choice.

DESIGN PRINCIPLES FOR EFFECTIVE LEADERSHIP DEVELOPMENT IN THE PUBLIC SECTOR

1. Real time, real work, real people

Bespoke leadership development interventions are designed with the participating organisation(s) around their real and current work effort, engaging with the people undertaking that work. The intervention starts with a current organisational issue, and enables the collective leadership capacity of those involved in that issue.

By 'real work', we mean the actual work the organisation is engaged on; a project or piece of work the participants are actively engaged on; or improving the actual relationships between work colleagues.

2. Start with 'what is'

Learning is effective when it is about real-time work, where the current real issues in the organisation are the 'case material' for the development activity. This means that there has to be an understanding amongst people taking part in the development activity about 'what is' – a shared reality of the current situation. This shared reality comes from exploring current behaviours – how we actually go about our work here.

We suggest that one way of accessing these behaviours is through stories. Telling stories about lived experiences in the organisation uncovers the current patterns of behaviour.

Whatever the approach, the current 'what is' picture needs to be one that is owned and shared across the organisation. Asking the person at the top is not enough, and doing it *for* the organisation rather than *with* the organisation will not work either.

3. Co-design the intervention with the participating organisation

You own what you create – any leadership intervention that is designed by the provider and the organisation will be 'owned' by both. It is more likely to have an impact within the organisation.

In addition, this process of co-design should be modelled in the real-time work that takes place, framed by the leadership development intervention.

4. Focus on the end-point – the impact for the user

For the intervention to be meaningful, it has to track back to the purpose of the organisation's work effort – the user. It has to demonstrate an impact on service offerings to service users.

5. Don't just talk about it – do it

Do real work as part of the intervention. Talking about work is not the same. The intervention has to lead to changes in behaviour.

6. Leave a legacy of real ongoing conversation in the organisation

The leaders taking part in the intervention develop their capacity for the processes being used in the intervention – for example, working with stories; processes for surfacing, and working with, differences; processes for listening – so that they can carry on using these processes at the end of the leadership development intervention.

7. Develop shared ambition

Shared ambition enables a wide range of leaders and potential leaders to make sense of the context in which they work, and to explore ways of shaping the future.

8. Make the most of difference and help understand multiple perspectives

The intervention must include processes that enable participants to learn about and understand other individuals' / professionals' / departments' ways of working and ways of understanding. It must make time for participants to step into each others' shoes and must challenge norms and assumptions (individual and organisational) about the viewpoints, motivations, and behaviours of others.

9. Amplify what works

The starting point for this principle is an appreciative stance that, in any organisation, things work to a degree, and that the task is to uncover and make more of these assets. Work with examples of promising practices locally to understand how to initiate, sustain, generate, develop and learn practices that support the organisation's core purpose.

10. Build understanding

The intervention must include ways of connecting the organisation to itself, to build people's understanding across the whole–spanning boundaries and hierarchies. Design interventions around systems issues, not just local issues, so that participants are engaging with members of a wider system than their immediate work-team. From a better understanding, trust may emerge.

11. Build possibilities and confidence

Possibilities are attractive to people, and working with what's possible (rather than what's not possible) energises people. Confidence is built through realising possibilities; providing a space in which mistakes generate learning; and designing personal, work and organisational feedback processes. Realising personal creativity, within the boundaries of the organisation's expectations of outcomes, generates innovation and identity. Connect the possibilities to the people in the organisation who have the authority to remove unnecessary hurdles.

12. Design innovative feedback processes into the leadership intervention

How do you know it is working? The intervention must include processes to review the impact of changed behaviours – for instance, peer review to connect others to the work. Develop personal and organisational feedback capability. Personal feedback – developing awareness of the impact individuals have on others in a range of work-teams. Feedback to the wider organisation's practices – develop congruency with organisational decision-making; reward systems; Find ways of testing newly-learnt behaviours and leadership practices – simulate; role-play; take on a real-time time-limited project.

13. Develop facilitative skills

Design interventions that enable the participants to learn listening and questioning skills.

14. Use conflict productively

Use difference and conflict more effectively to foster a culture that learns from conflict, uses it to reach different possibilities and harnesses the capabilities of the whole of the organisation.

15. The leadership development intervention is core business

To generate wide organisational impact, embed the leadership development activity in the organisation's systems and processes – for example, appraisal and decision-making. This requires whole organisational commitment to the intervention, and top-team consideration of learning from the intervention.

16. Seek external perturbation

Use the leadership development process as a way of generating challenge to the leaders' and organisation's current thinking, ways of operating, and ways of organising, by seeking challenge from external sources.

CASE EXAMPLE 3

LEADERSHIP IN THE PUBLIC SECTOR

SHARING & HELPING: CROSS-ORGANISATIONAL LOCAL GOVERNMENT COACHING / MENTORING

The North East Regional Employers' Organisation (NEREO) launched a coaching / mentoring programme for human resources (HR) professionals in local government in the North East in 2005-2006. This took place alongside a number of other initiatives in which NEREO was involved, all designed to help to develop the HR function in local government.

The aim of the programme was to help individual HR practitioners to meet the challenges facing them, and to develop their professional and leadership abilities. The programme was intended for people who were moving into new positions and facing new challenges, or those who were considering how to take the next step in their career. The programme was designed to pair experienced HR professionals, who would provide coaching / mentoring support, with more junior and / or less-experienced HR practitioners. A key element of the design was that people would be paired with partners from different organisations.

NEREO administered the scheme, sought senior HR professionals who would be willing to act as coaches / mentors, and recruited practitioners who thought they would benefit from coaching / mentoring. NEREO also employed an external consultant to provide initial training, and to co-ordinate the programme.

Six experienced HR professionals took part in an initial meeting, and agreed the detailed design of the programme. This initial meeting also included some training for the coaches / mentors in relevant skills and techniques. The discussion on the design of the programme led to the agreement of ground rules on key issues (see the panel below). It was agreed that an important part of the programme was that the coaches / mentors would help participants to make their own decisions about the issues that faced them, taking a non-directive, facilitative approach. There is much debate about the terms 'coaching' and 'mentoring', and the similarities and differences between the two but, for simplicity, the group decided to call the programme the 'HR Coaching Programme'.

The training element of the meeting provided some knowledge inputs / reminders on the nature of coaching, mentoring and learning, and on different coaching and mentoring styles, and included some ideas and activities to help to develop facilitation skills.

The programme was publicised through the North East local authorities' HR network, and a number of practitioners put their names forward to participate. A further three coaches were drawn into the programme, and all nine coaches were paired with a participant. The matching process took into account locations and job roles, and the need to pair participants with coaches from organisations other than their own. In all, 12 organisations, including NEREO, took part in the programme, providing one or more coaches or participants. There were some minor problems in matching coaches and participants – in two instances, participants wanted coaches who had experience in their own particular area of HR – but, on the whole, the matching process went smoothly.

GROUND RULES

This is a summary of the ground rules agreed for the programme. A more detailed set of statements was developed and issued to coaches and participants.

Roles: What each party would do
It was agreed that the coach's role was to help participants to make their own decisions and develop their abilities, through a mixture of support, guidance and challenge.

Coaches agreed to:

- Listen to participants, be non-judgemental, have an open mind.
- Help participants to think things through, resolve problems, find solutions, and develop their skills.
- Share their experiences with participants when that appeared to be helpful and appropriate.
- If it seemed appropriate, provide information, or contacts, or suggest people or sources of information participants might consult.

Participants were expected to:

- Have some ideas about what they would like to work on, and what they would like to gain from the activity.
- Have an open mind, be willing to consider different approaches to issues.

Confidentiality
Discussions between the coach and participant were confidential.

Basics
Basic arrangements for the programme were expressed as 'default positions': for example, the proposed length of the programme was 12 months, but it was open to the coach and participant, by mutual agreement, to meet over a shorter or a longer period of time. It was stated that meetings would probably take place once a month, would last for an hour or an hour-and-a-half, and would take place at the coach's organisation. Pairs were given licence to alter these arrangements by mutual agreement (in practice, it turned out, most pairs followed these defaults).

Contingencies
It was agreed that if the relationship was not working, or if participants felt that they were not benefiting from the programme as they expected, they should raise this with their coach in the first instance, and seek to agree what to do. Coaches and participants were encouraged to contact the programme co-ordinator if issues could not be resolved, or if any further problems arose.

EVALUATION

The programme was evaluated six months after the coaches started working with their participants, and again after 12 months. Questionnaires were issued to coaches and participants on both occasions by the programme co-ordinator.

Responses from the participants indicated that the scheme was very successful. All respondents said that they were 'satisfied' or 'very satisfied' with the programme.

Comments included:

- *'I have received exceptional advice, guidance and support from my coach. I really feel inspired and motivated when I leave the sessions.'*
- *'Helps me to reflect upon my actions, consider how I might have done things differently and how to cope with hypothetical repercussions of my actions.'*
- *'The coach can also make you think about possibilities or consequences of an action that you maybe cannot see when you are too close to something.'*
- *'I feel this has been a positive experience for me and the process is working well.'*

At the end of the 12 months, most participants said they would like to negotiate with their coach to continue to meet for the next six months, in some cases meeting less frequently than before. The coaches all agreed that they would be willing to carry on working with their participant (and some continued to do so over a year later).

Coaches' responses to the evaluations indicated their own gains, including:

- Experience and insight into the processes of coaching / mentoring / facilitating others to make decisions.
- Perspectives on HR in other organisations

A concern on the part of prospective coaches in such a scheme is often the amount of their time it will take. In this scheme, most pairs met roughly once a month, with meetings lasting between one and two hours. Most coaches found that they needed about an extra half-hour, in addition to the time spent in the meeting, for preparation or follow-up. There was little in the way of discussion by email or telephone between meetings. The time demands, therefore, were quite manageable.

Coaches and participants both agreed that it was useful to work with someone from the same profession, but from a different organisation.

In a review meeting, the coaches discussed how the programme could be improved. The participants held a range of positions in HR, from senior to junior levels and, although all individual participants had benefited from the programme, the coaches thought that it might have more impact on the HR function and capacity across the region if it was more clearly focused on two groups:

- New heads of HR, who could be paired with an experienced head from another organisation.
- HR professionals who had recently taken on team leader or manager responsibilities, or who were on the verge of doing so.

CASE EXAMPLE 4

CITY LEADERSHIP FORUM, MANCHESTER

The City Leadership Forum is a practical intervention for leaders, primarily across public services, in Manchester. The Forum provides leaders with a space to meet informally to share leadership practice and to develop different ways of thinking to address the practical challenges of leading, for the strategic benefit of Manchester and the Greater Manchester area. The City Leadership Forum is hosted by Manchester City Council, working in partnership with Manchester Metropolitan University. It has been sponsored by the HEFCE Innovation Funding, the North West Regional Development Agency, Manchester Metropolitan University Business School and the Northern Leadership Academy.

CONTEXT

The Forum, founded by Susan Kirkcaldy, is part of a research project at Manchester Metropolitan University, aimed at promoting and supporting leadership, enterprise and innovation in the city. Susan's work focuses expanding the capacity for creativity, innovation and new ways of thinking that are of practical benefit to leaders in complex situations. A specific objective within this particular project was to encourage partnerships between academics and practitioners to support the growth of the city and the region.

INTERVENTION

The first City Leadership Forum was held in September 2006, with a second in April 2007. Further events are planned for 2008. Each event was limited to between 60 and 70 leaders, mostly CEOs and directors, from across public services, with some key private sector companies. These included: local government, police, fire, prisons, health, education, as well as arts, architecture and media, with information technology, science and technology, law and financial services, human resource development and a variety of development and regeneration organisations.

Susan led a team from Manchester Metropolitan University, working in partnership with the Head of Leadership & Organisation Development at Manchester City Council, and her team. The City Leadership Forum team worked for many months prior to the Forum event to develop the idea of the Forum and to build a constituency of support for its purpose, along with consulting on the detailed format, content themes, keynote presenters and participants. Participating leaders were individually invited by Sir Howard Bernstein, CEO of Manchester City Council.

Each event has followed a similar simple format. The Forums were held at the end of the working day, at the Manchester Midland Hotel in the heart of the city centre. The Forums began with an informal networking reception. At the start, there were a number of short presentations: one from the Vice-Chancellor of Manchester Metropolitan University, who introduced the event; a second from a representative of Manchester City Council; and the third from the academic sponsors.

What followed was an interactive presentation from a keynote presenter. This part of the Forum provided external challenge and 'thought leadership' from an experienced practitioner and academic, to provide input on current thinking in leadership theory and to stimulate discussion on how this supports the practical work of leading. After a period of discussion across the full participant group, conversations continued in table groups over dinner, when participating leaders were encouraged to debate the issues of their own leadership practice in the context of the main discussion theme. All participating leaders also were given a personal copy of a key leadership book that related directly to the keynote presentation. The Forums were closed with a summary of key points by the Dean of Manchester Metropolitan University Business School.

At the first City Leadership Forum, Professor John Brookes, Vice-Chancellor of Manchester Metropolitan University spoke about the importance of academics working in partnership with leaders across Manchester in the development of the city, particularly in the context of the Manchester agenda as a 'knowledge capital'. Sir Howard Bernstein, CEO of Manchester City Council, spoke about 'pioneering leadership in Manchester' for the development of the city. Susan herself talked about her own research into the realities of developing new ways of thinking to address the practical challenges of leading, from which the idea of the City Leadership Forum was generated, on behalf of one of the business schools within the city of Manchester.

The keynote presenter at the first Forum was Mike Pedler, Professor of Action Learning at Henley Management College. He led a participative session on 'Collaborative Leadership & Action Learning in Public Services'. Mike used practical examples from the leaders present to demonstrate the value of the action learning method to create new pragmatic responses to practical problems and to explore the nature and purpose of leading, as experienced by those leaders who were present.

At the second event, Professor John Brookes spoke further about the importance of 'collaborative partnerships between the academic community and public service and private sector organisations for the benefit of the city's sustainable growth'. On this occasion, he was followed by the Deputy CEO of Manchester City Council, Mike Reardon, who stressed 'the need to build links with the Business School... to feed on the knowledge in business schools to support the city'. He outlined the challenges in the changing face of Manchester, 'Manchester is recognised as a knowledge economy, with a new role as a post-industrial city to support knowledge workers.' The academic head of the 'think-tank', Richard Thorpe, then explained the purpose and role of the Northern Leadership Academy in fostering better leadership across the North of England and in supporting the City Leadership Forum initiative.

This was followed by a keynote presentation from Irwin Turbitt, Senior Associate Fellow at the Institute of Governance & Public

Management, at Warwick University Business School. Irwin was previously Assistant Chief Constable of the Police Service for Northern Ireland, and Home Office Adviser. He led a highly-challenging and thought-provoking presentation on 'adaptive leadership'. For Irwin, adaptive leadership is all about leaders creating the conditions for everyone involved in an issue to learn to respond to its resolution. He stated that his purpose, and that of the City Leadership Forum, was 'to move to a new place, a new level of thinking'. This was a thoughtful and provocative presentation that led to a robust debate amongst the leaders present.

OUTCOMES

The two City Leadership Forums have both proved extremely successful and influential, in terms of receiving overwhelming positive support from those participating, and from many unable to participate, who wished to do so. All feedback, formal and informal, has indicated the value of a Forum for senior leaders across the city to discuss the challenges of their own practice and to expand their thinking about leadership, in the context of the City development agenda. People spoke of the benefits of 'new networks of relationships and interests' and of 'the cross-over into a range of different contexts on numerous projects in the city'.

There was a huge buzz of interest in continuing to support this initiative. Most comments concentrated on the potential value of the Forum: 'they have real potential'; are 'really useful'; and also 'offers excellent opportunities', which provide the possibility of developing a 'powerful public private sector partnership for Manchester'.

Leaders who participated in one or both of these events have been active in suggesting how to sustain and improve the benefits of the Forum. The focus of the majority is to expand the opportunity for informal networking, as well as the 'thought leadership' interaction. There are various specific recommendations on all aspects of the Forum, including the format, frequency, time and timing. Mostly, people were looking for 'more regular contact', as 'meeting infrequently makes it difficult to build links'.

There is considerable debate about the mix of participants, with two clear themes. First, for the Forum to fulfil its function, the participating leaders need to be peers, 'sharing experiences on crucial issues was very positive', so that building relationships and understanding is developed over time. For many, the Forum 'is serving its function of bringing together the Manchester leaders who are now beginning to build friendship and trust'.

Second, there is a difference in views regarding the mix of participating leaders. For some, a key value lies in an exclusively public service Leadership Forum. It is 'a great opportunity to meet with a range of people from across public sector organisations in the city' and most useful was developing 'a better perspective on city leadership issues'. For others, the value lies in a greater balance of public service and private sector leaders from across the city: 'it was good to see the challenges of leadership being addressed in a collaborative way across so many fields'. A key benefit was developing 'shared perspectives across boundaries and interest groups' and 'building understanding across different interest groups', as well as simply a 'good opportunity to create links with others'.

The intention of the City Leadership Forum was to create a space for leaders to meet and to discuss practical leadership issues outside of the remit of specific project meetings. For some, the Forum could develop usefully into a context specifically to explore city-wide challenges. For others, the Forum is more useful as a crucible for learning from 'new ideas debated' and 'encouraging to think from the viewpoint of the big picture'.

The keynote presenters provided an external challenge, which had a mixed response, particularly in the second Forum. For some, the discussions of a 'challenging nature' were uncomfortable, people were 'not sure the ... approach was appropriate to the audience' and some felt the style was 'antagonising / discomforting a considerable number of those present' and 'the presentation was provocative in the extreme'. Others appreciated this challenge: 'very good – really liked the approach and ideas generated', which was considered, 'refreshing' and 'thought-provoking' by others. Providing an external challenge in this arena proved to be a matter of fine balance.

Extending the 'thought-leadership' contribution by distributing personal copies of books was universally appreciated: 'the book was a valuable bonus, an opportunity to look into the issues raised further' and 'being given the book to take away and read has been really helpful to me in developing a more enhanced understanding of adaptive leadership and having time to reflect and apply the theory to my work'.

The City Leadership Forum was conceived originally to create a space for leaders in Manchester to engage in conversations with their peers about the personal challenges of leading in the city. A central theme also was to provide 'thought-leadership', to expand the possibilities of leadership thinking and to inform leadership practice. Creating space for this kind of practical peer conversation amongst senior leaders from across the range of public services takes a long time to get off the ground with different interest groups and requires dedicated leadership and funding to generate maximum benefits for city leaders.

The first Forum was a 'one-off' experiment that was extended on the basis of the success it generated amongst all those participating – that is, individual leaders and sponsoring organisations. Following the success of the second Forum, there was a commitment given to sustain the Forum concept at least on an annual basis. The City Leadership Forum is currently part – albeit a minor part – of both main partnership organisations' ongoing leadership initiatives: Manchester Metropolitan University Business School is pioneering leadership research and development programmes in the city, while Manchester City Council is fully engaged in internal leadership development programmes at all leadership levels and is keen to promote practical opportunities for informal networking and supporting leadership in the city – especially across all public services.

SUMMARY

'Developing leadership practice', of course, is a central concern for all the participating leaders and within the organisations they lead and represent. In summary, the participants' comments from these Forums suggest that creating a dedicated space for senior leaders to build understanding across multiple organisations and different sectors delivers practical learning that makes a difference and has the potential to contribute to the future of leadership practice in the city and represents a good example of a leadership development approach that is membership-based, where all those attending can learn from each other, particularly in areas where service provision is becoming closely inter-related.

10

APPROACHING THE VOLUNTARY SECTOR

I n this chapter, we investigate what is known in relation to leadership programmes / interventions that work in support of distributed leadership in the voluntary and community sectors (VCS). We report the results of the NLA's efforts to develop a set of principles to guide our practice of what works for voluntary sector organisations. These principles are:

- Engage with the identity, values and interests of the leader.
- Recognise that service users and service providers may be the same people.
- Understand the political, social and historical context of the VCS and its relationship with other sectors.
- Understand the diversity of the VCS.
- Identify and support what is distinctive about community leaders.
- Develop the VCS as a sector.
- Ensure high quality training.
- Recognise and support the integrated strategic role of VCS leaders.

INTRODUCTION

The principles detailed in this chapter have derived from the findings of a scoping exercise, which maps the leadership development experience and needs of community leaders in the Northern region. A key question which arose from this scoping process is "who exactly are community leaders?". The term 'community leader' has a broad range of meanings and associations, all of which are valid in their different contexts, but may be very diverse and even contradictory. For example, community leaders are democratically-elected members of local government and have a formal mandate to represent their community's interests and views. Community leaders also are those who consciously stand outside of elected democratic structures and specifically represent their community to elected leaders or even act in opposition to elected community leaders.

For the purposes of this discussion, community leaders are those who exercise leadership outside of public and private sector organisations. They may be elected political leaders; employees of a VCS organisation; volunteers; tenant or community-based representatives; or they may be individuals living and working on the margins of mainstream social frameworks and taking up a leadership role in whatever community they find themselves within.

The scoping work included:

- Two diagnostic café-style events, held in Sheffield and Newcastle, attracting over 70 people to explore the questions of community leadership. These events were co-hosted by the Centre for Innovation in Health Management and local groups or organisations that reflect some of the diversity of community leadership systems. A number of people working within the public and private sectors also were invited to the events, in order to ensure that ideas and experience from the whole system of community leadership were reflected in the discussions.
- A broad range of telephone and face-to-face conversations with community leaders and their partners took place, allowing some of the subtleties and painful personal difficulties of community leadership to be included in this scoping of the issues.

- Desk-based research into national policy frameworks and existing local / regional research on community leadership.

Using the principles

We offer these as a starting point for both providers of leadership interventions and readers seeking to commission leadership development work in their sector.

A note on language

We use the term 'leadership development intervention' rather than 'leadership development programme' as the background work demonstrated the need for a range of leadership development activity. 'Programmes' usually conjures up ideas of workshops, classrooms, off-site sessions, time-outs and personal development diagnostics. 'Interventions' offers more of a spectrum, from individual development to organisational development – giving more choice.

DESIGN PRINCIPLES FOR WHAT WORKS IN VOLUNTARY & COMMUNITY SECTOR LEADERSHIP DEVELOPMENT

1. Engage with the identity, values and interests of the leader

For community leaders, learning becomes meaningful when it is strongly related to their concerns, problems, values and desires. It is important to explore the personal and social context of their leadership and the story of how they come to be in their leadership role. The work of many community leaders grows out of a personal concern for justice or commitment to the people of their communities and, therefore, is closely connected to their personal values or principles. Keeping this personal and professional connection to the fore in leadership development is important.

2. Recognise that service users and service providers may be the same people

Whilst many of the people employed by VCS organisations have the same personal needs as the average citizen, a distinguishing feature of the VCS leadership spectrum is that service providers and service users are often the same people and, unlike the public sector, where clear lines are drawn between service users and service providers, this factor needs to be acknowledged and addressed in training for community leaders.

3. Understand the political, social and historical context of the VCS and its relationship with other sectors

The VCS traditionally has been a second cousin in the delivery of services and its 'voluntary' status has often created an impression (and also a reality) of amateur, low-cost, non-essential and unprofessional service delivery. The historical, political role of the VCS also is importunate here, particularly in relation to power dynamics with the public and private sector, on whom funding for VCS work usually is dependent. The current changing profile of the VCS as a 'third sector' needs to be understood in this context, both in relation to the identity of VCS leaders and in relation to the interpersonal dynamics between partners across the old sector boundaries, who now theoretically compete on a level playing field.

4. Understand the diversity of the VCS

The VCS is not a homogenous body or sector; it is highly diverse, comprising large, formal organisations and institutions on the one hand, and individual activists and local leaders on the other. The VCS covers communities of interest (for example, disability), as well as geographical and ethnic origin communities. It also cuts across formal democratic leadership (for example, elected councillors) and non-democratic local leadership (for example, residents' groups). The specific, and yet very diverse, needs of this spectrum of community leadership needs must be understood and addressed in any training for VCS leaders.

5. Identify and support what is distinctive about community leadership

Community leaders often see themselves as distinct from leaders in other sectors. This is important to their identity, but the distinctiveness is often not articulated or consciously developed. Understanding and exploring notions of community leadership in relation to generic notions of leadership is important in the current climate of third sector development, if the distinctiveness of a third sector is to be retained, and if assimilation of the VCS into the public and private sectors is to be avoided.

If there is anything distinctive about community leadership, how can this be articulated and consciously developed? What can be borrowed or adapted from other forms of leadership and contemporary thinking about leadership to enhance VCS leadership? These are important questions to foreground in any leadership development work with community leaders.

6. Develop the VCS as a sector

The diversity of the VCS often creates fragmentation, competition and a lack of coherence in terms of the collective voice of the sector. Although there has been recent investment in supporting VCS infrastructure, there are still considerable isolation and communication difficulties within the sector itself. It is important to use every training programme as a dual opportunity to enhance the personal skills of individuals, whilst, at the same time, creating communities of practice, where peer learning and relationships can be developed within the sector, leading to a more coherent, networked entity.

7. Ensure high quality training

The VCS often has been on the receiving end of low-cost, low-quality training. In part, this is the result of historical under-investment in VCS training, assumptions about the 'voluntary' nature of the work – 'do the best we can with what we've got', rather than planning properly for quality investment – and also partly due to assumptions about the 'second cousin' nature of VCS work and the lower priority often given to supporting its work. The need for ensuring that VCS training is of the same quality and aspiration as training for leaders in other sectors in an important principle, if the VCS is to play a full and equitable role in our society as a viable third sector.

8. Recognise and support the integrated strategic role of VCS leaders

Many VCS leaders are required to work, not just with their local communities, but also with strategic partners in other sectors and organisations. Their role often is a brokering one, though they also are required to contribute both to local strategic agendas and to nationally-driven changes to the third sector role in service delivery. There is a need for sector-specific support for VCS leaders operating at a strategic level, but there is also a need for reflective learning opportunities and development of advanced leadership and communication skills for leaders across the sectors. This includes supporting the capacity of statutory partners and commissioners to work more creatively with the multiplicity of VCS providers that current policy changes will produce. The principle of ensuring that the whole system of strategic social leadership is included in any VCS training is just as important as ensuring that the role of the VCS is included in any leadership training for public and private sector leaders.

LEARNING ABOUT STATUTORY ORGANISATIONS FROM ENGAGING WITH THE VOLUNTARY & COMMUNITY SECTOR

Our learnings included:

- That the VCS has information, which is valuable and necessary for the delivery of NLA objectives in relation to leadership development in Northern regions. It should not be assumed that this knowledge is free knowledge or that the VCS has the time, the resource or the desire to help us with our agenda by taking part in scoping exercises or consultation events.

- It is important to ensure mutuality of benefit to all parties involved, recognising the value of the knowledge that VCS leaders bring to our agenda and treating it as a resource to be valued and purchased in the same way as any other knowledge source (academic, business, consultants, etc.) In practical terms, this might mean paying VCS advisers as consultants, and / or identifying a local issue to be addressed through the process.

- Co-creation – working with an established local community partner to develop and co-host the process – generates credibility and ownership locally, but also requires a process of relationship-building and investing in developing the co-host partnership.

- An appropriate approach for engaging in needs assessment or scoping processes is the dual task approach, which identifies the needs of target communities, whilst at the same time developing the capacity of that community to shape and own the interventions and subsequent outcomes that arise. This is an active participation model, rather than a representative or public consultation model.

- Developing an integrated process that values both the knowledge and experience of local people and also of professionals from across the sectors who work with VCS.

- Recognising that communities operate within a diverse social system – with myriad interests, agendas and knowledge bases – which needs to be approached on a holistic basis, rather than as a series of fragmented or disconnected issues and activities.

- Recognising and respecting the differences between communities and groups within the VCS, even amongst those that are apparently quite similar.

- Co-learning by using models and techniques that deliver the core task of gathering information, and which may also contribute something to the learning and capacity of VCS groups – for example, sharing information on how to use café-style community events within the VCS leadership scoping events.

- During the scoping phase, to model the principles, practice and commitment we would bring to the leadership development interventions.

- The process of engagement must take account of the deficit of experience and aspiration that is often a cause of exclusion in marginalised or deprived communities. The process, therefore, needs to be highly-supportive, flexible, aspirational and responsive. Consultation activities that fail to address this deficit of experience are likely to generate inaccurate or inadequate findings. If these are then used as the basis for building future strategies, the end result often is an irrelevant process or a service that is inaccessible and fails to meet needs.

THE NLA SCOPING EXERCISE, WITH REPRESENTATION FROM THE SECTOR

Our scoping exercise work, mapping the leadership development experience and needs of community leaders in the Northern region, collected the views and experiences of a wide range of managers and leaders in voluntary sector organisations. This process also has generated a number of conclusions about themes that could usefully be incorporated into NLA leadership programmes; information about the support needs of community leaders that should be addressed in any future interventions; and ideas for developing leadership in the Northern area. These are outlined in the following sections.

THEMES & ISSUES FOR COMMUNITY LEADERS

- **Notions of leadership:** Is there anything distinctive about community leadership? How can this be articulated and consciously developed? What can be borrowed or adapted from other forms of leadership and contemporary thinking about leadership to enhance VCS leadership?

- **Sector development:** What are the issues that underpin development of the 'sector' in Northern regions and what organisational and sector-based infrastructure building needs to take place?

- **VCS role in mainstream policy development and service delivery:** How can the third sector develop a viable role within current policy and delivery opportunities without losing the distinctiveness of its 'third sector' identity? In particular, how can the specific experience of leaders from deprived or marginalised communities, including refugee and asylum-seeker communities, be understood better, developed and accessed to the benefit of mainstream agendas?

- **Policy-planning and decision-making:** How can VCS groups engage in policy-planning and decision-making – for example, about the needs of deprived and marginalised communities – in a way that goes beyond consultation or participation in the current structures and facilitates a more systemic appraisal of the decision-making process.

- **Leading partnerships together:** How can VCS leaders come together with leaders from other sectors to explore the implications of integrated 'partnership leadership'? A distributed model of leadership has particular appeal in this context, but what would it look like in a diverse cross-sector context that is mutually owned by all the stakeholders? Exploring these issues *via* practical initiatives, such as new commissioning strategies for social enterprises, would be a creative and topical way of doing this.

- **Power:** What are the power dynamics underpinning the relationship between VCS leaders and leaders from other sectors? Is there a hidden professionalisation agenda? Similarly, what are the power dynamics within the diversity of the VCS itself – between asylum-seeker and BME communities, between community activists and voluntary sector organisations?

- **Personal needs and context of community leaders:** How can the significant personal needs of many community leaders be addressed in leadership programmes?

- **Practical work-based learning:** How can leadership development programmes balance the need for technical and practical workplace support with a reflective whole systems approach to learning and personal development?

- **Young people:** How can the energy and ideas of young people be combined more effectively with the experience and maturity of adults? How can we support leadership development in young leaders, both to learn more about notions of leadership, and to support them in their preparation for adult leadership roles?

THE SUPPORT NEEDS OF VOLUNTARY & COMMUNITY SECTOR LEADERS IN TRAINING & DEVELOPMENT PROGRAMMES

The leadership development experience of community leaders emerging from this scoping process suggests that the following issues need to be taken into account in the provision of any future NLA interventions:

- Support for personal circumstances and the complexities of being a leader in deprived or socially-excluded communities. This might mean the provision of programmes specifically geared to the needs of leaders from within these communities, and / or it might mean consciously taking account of these needs in general programmes.

- Support for the specific, and more strategic, level of need experienced by leaders and managers of VCS organisations.

- Emphasis on high quality, both in terms of environment and facilitation.

- Practical issues: training opportunities needs to be accessible for participants with limited personal or organisational resources – for example, in terms of cost and time.

- More opportunities for experiential, personal development training and less focus on theoretical, content-based and technical training.

- An emphasis on confidence-building, sustaining self and managing relationships is needed across the sector – for local leaders / activists, leaders of community organisations and more senior leaders.

- Practically-based: focusing on real (not theoretical) work and community issues, and which are as much about creating meaning as problem-solving.

- Training programmes must be cognisant of, and appropriate to, the wider power dynamics within communities, and between different sectors and government. The question of professionalisation of community leaders and the wider systemic implications of the mainstreaming agenda are key themes here.

- Networking objectives: Programmes need to contribute to strengthening the sector objectives, as well as strengthening individuals. Opportunities for peer learning and information exchange are important in this respect.

- There is a need for trainers and facilitators who have experience and expertise in working with the voluntary sector, and also the subtleties and complexities of leaders from marginalised or deprived communities. There is potential for developing new career paths and employment opportunities for VCS leaders within the leadership development sector.

- Incorporating key strategic themes and issues into the programme – for example, commissioning agenda and social enterprise developments – and using these as opportunities for exploring the practical and personal implications, as much as an opportunity for information input. This could be facilitated by inviting contributions from people in other sectors into the programme, and / or by offering a programme that consciously sets out to bring together a mixed group of leaders to explore the implications of leading these initiatives together.

Proposed NLA Future Support for Voluntary & Community Sector Leaders

A number of ideas and proposals emerged from the scoping exercise that the NLA could develop as a means to support leadership development in the VCS. These include:

- Leadership development programmes for community activists and local leaders.

- An integrated leadership development programme for people working in partnerships across the sectors, particularly in public sector and VCS partnerships.

- A programme for young people and adults, exploring the learning for leadership, which could be generated from cross-generational interventions.

- A leadership programme for refugee and asylum-seeker leaders, exploring what is the distinctive contribution of leaders from refugee communities and how this can be a more effective resource in UK mainstream policy and service delivery.

- Learning sets that support peer learning in depth and in an ongoing capacity.

- Networking and learning events that help to strengthen the sector and to maintain peer learning. This to be linked with the work of the Engaging Communities in Leadership (ECL) network, a research-based network bringing people together from "all areas and levels of public sector, university faculty and local business who pool their relevant knowledge and connections to realise initiatives that will shape both specific tasks and positive changes for the North West as a whole".[74]

- Train-the-trainer programmes for leadership development facilitators from public or private sector training providers who want to facilitate programmes in a VCS context; and programmes for VCS practitioners who want to use their sector-specific knowledge in a facilitation and learning development context. This programme would have the dual aim of building skills and employment capacity within the VCS and other sectors, as well as raising the standard and quality of leadership development intervention for community leaders.

It is recommended that:

- The follow-up stage to the scoping phase should concentrate on two prototype leadership programmes: one for community activists and one for senior leaders across the public sectors and VCS. Potential community leader facilitators should be identified in this process and involved in the knowledge capture and facilitation process, where possible.

---

[74]   Lancaster Leadership Centre (2005). *Engaging Communities in Leadership: The Voice of the Future* conference, September, Lancaster: Lancaster Leadership Centre.

- The learning from these prototypes should be captured and fed into the NLA strategy for supporting leadership capacity in the VCS.

- Development work is undertaken to explore funding and options for the young people and adults programme, the refugee leaders' programme, train-the-trainers programmes and a leadership learning network for VCS leaders – for example, a series of master-classes on key topics that pick up on the themes emerging from the above and are available to a wider audience.

CASE EXAMPLE 5

LEADERSHIP IN THE VOLUNTARY SECTOR

LEEDS MIND

Leeds Mind is a voluntary agency affiliated to Mind (the National Association for Mental Health). It supports people with mental health problems, offering a diverse range of services, including counselling, day-care, housing, employment, self-help group work and information and training facilities. It aims to change the way people with mental health problems are seen, to reduce the prejudice and discrimination against them and to enable them to lead rich and rewarding lives that contribute positively to their communities. Leeds Mind is committed to developing innovative and effective services that promote mental health for the people in Leeds.

Governance of Leeds Mind is co-ordinated by an Executive Committee, which provides an accountability framework for the often-complicated and demanding work undertaken alongside people with mental health problems. The work of the Executive Committee is largely strategic, focusing upon the direction of the organisation, its public profile and resources.

The NLA design principles for what works in voluntary and community organisations have resonance for Leeds Mind, and are articulated in its core values document. This provides an outline for shared understanding and commitment across the organisation for working practices and supporting service users. The values, in no specific priority order, are as follows:

- **All human beings have mental health needs:** One in four people will experience mental health problems at some point and the dividing line between 'the sane' and 'the mad' is artificial and demeaning to all people. It is important to pay attention to, and take care of, our mental health needs and to challenge the stigma and prejudice.

- **We recognise that there are multiple causes of mental health problems and that different interventions can be effective :** The medical model locates 'the fault' in the person with 'the problems' and we are critical of this. We recognise that social and environmental stresses (for example, poverty, racism, and abuse) have negative impacts that can result in mental health problems. We are committed to challenging the imbalances in power that often reinforce and result in mental health problems. Increasing choice for service users is an important part of what we do and this is part of putting power into people's hands.

- **All people have the capacity to recover from mental health problems:** We recognise that the word 'recovery' is not perfect, but believe that people have the ability to discover in themselves what they need to do to improve the condition of their lives. Our role is to help people build on the resources they already have to achieve their own desired outcomes.

- **We recognise the central importance of human relationships:** Relationships are valuable because they play a central role in many people's recovery. Positive relationships recognise and respect the whole person, practically, intellectually, emotionally, spiritually and socially.

- **We have a profound respect for the capabilities and resourcefulness of service users:** We value their input at all levels in the organisation and see our task as facilitating creative alliances between service users and workers that maximise positive outcomes for service users. We work hard to reduce the artificial barriers between those two roles.

- **Our staff and volunteers are the organisation's major resource:** We value the time, energy and commitment that staff and volunteers give to us. We endeavour to support staff and volunteers to undertake the difficult work we ask them to do. We endeavour to reward and enable people to develop positively in order to fulfil their potential and we respect the creativity that they bring to their work.

- **We value diversity and are committed to celebrating it in all its dimensions:** We aspire to acknowledge and value diversity and difference and actively seek to challenge and correct imbalances of power and the negative impacts of oppression and discrimination.

- **We endeavour to work to the best of our ability:** We are committed to celebrating our successes, understanding our mistakes and value the importance of what we can learn from them.

- **As an organisation, we aspire to a culture of openness:** We try to create the best conditions in which issues can be directly addressed and more fully understood. We encourage all people to take responsibility for themselves and to act as autonomous agents within a supportive framework.

- **All our services endeavour to empower people:** The aim of our work is to help people build on their strengths, overcome obstacles and become more in control of their lives. Our services seek to improve the experience of people with mental health problems and we are committed to developing effective and innovative projects which promote change for the better.

Julian Turner, chief executive of Leeds Mind, has indicated that recognition and support for diversity in the sector is an important element to consider when developing any leadership-type provision. Drawing together collections of different strands of support and delivery in the sector enables connectedness to develop effectively:

> *'One practical way of illustrating the underlying connectedness between the diverse strands is to get people to seek commonalities between communities. For instance, the stigma of mental health labels and the impact of racism. This can highlight differences and samenesses.'*

Related to the issue of 'connectedness' between organisations is identity. In the voluntary and community sector, problems and issues can arise for leaders if they mistake their own journey with the cause they are representing. For Julian, a wish for people to be able to take more control of their own lives has been a motivating driver throughout his whole working life:

> *'If I confuse my own narrative with that of the cause, I will be far less effective. A capacity for "other-focused-ness" is a requirement that should form part of leadership provision for those in this sector'.*

PART 3:
TAKING LEADERSHIP DEVELOPMENT FORWARD

11

THE PRINCIPLES OF
EVIDENCE–LED LEADERSHIP

I *n this chapter, we explore the nature of leadership development provision available to those charged with leading organisations.*

Leadership development providers are becoming increasingly aware of the need to design and deliver learning interventions that add value to a business or an organisation. An element of our work within the Northern Leadership Academy has been concerned with examining how the evaluation of development activity, in itself, can influence the impact of learning.

Our model of evaluation-led leadership development characterises evaluation as an activity integrated into the whole process, rather than something carried out as a separate activity at the end of a project.

In constructing this approach, we have developed a set of questions that may assist leadership development providers to build evaluation into their learning interventions and to place the learner at the centre of the process.

What Do We Mean by 'Leadership & Management Development'?

The term 'management education' is used to describe activities aimed at providing learning opportunities for managers, usually in universities and other higher education institutions. 'Management and leadership development' is a much wider concept, which can encompass both the idea of manager or leaders becoming better at what they do, by acquiring new skills and knowledge, and the idea of developing a managerial career.

'Management training' is now a term that is infrequently used and is usually subsumed under the heading of management development. When the term management training is used, it is normally to describe a process in which management or leadership is broken down into its component parts (for example, managing time; managing people; handling conflict) and delivered in individual 'chunks'. It becomes more significant when these skills and attitudes are viewed holistically, rather than as a set of individual attributes which can be acquired. Learning to be a leader takes much more than knowing the 'how to'; it is about being able to apply this technical knowledge in a particular context and being able to understand the whole set of concepts together. It is rather like thinking that you can learn to drive a car by knowing how to operate the brakes, accelerator and steering wheel, without putting all of these components together and driving in a range of road conditions.

In this chapter, when we talk about leadership development, we are concerned with helping leaders and managers to acquire the component parts of the management role and to be sensitive to the context and culture in which they are operating and to focus on their own self-development.

Leadership development brings benefits to the individual, to the organisation, or to both concurrently. There are times when development activities may focus more heavily either on the individual or the business but, ideally, both sets of needs can be identified, met and evaluated.

WHAT IS THE BEST WAY TO DEVELOP LEADERS?

Here, it might be useful to see what the UK government thinks is the right way to develop leaders. Looking back on government action over the past 20 years, it is clear that that leadership development is considered to be a matter for concern and debate. In the mid-1980s, various reports identified that managers in the UK received little or no formal training and this was considered to be a major impediment to national and regional economic success.

Two significant reports were published in 1987, both reviewing the parlous state of British management education and development and suggesting a way forward. Charles Handy's *The Making of Managers*, published in 1987, provides a review of management education and development in competitor countries (USA, West Germany, France and Japan). The main conclusion from this review was that Britain did not have a clearly signposted and accepted education and development process for managers, unlike other nations which, although different in each of their approaches, had some kind of structure. Handy concluded that:

> *'There can be little doubt that, by comparison with the other countries in this study, Britain has neglected her managerial stock.'*[75]

Handy recommended the development and delivery of new management qualifications and the establishment of a 'Charter Group', which eventually became the lead body for management qualifications under the NVQ regime. It is in this area of vocational qualifications that the Handy Report had most influence. There is now a clear framework of management qualifications, many of which can be gained by accrediting prior learning. However, this only provides us with the technical part of being a manager, and not the contextual awareness and sensing elements that enable managers to become leaders.

---

[75]   Handy, C. (1987). *The Making of Managers: Report on the Management Education, Training & Development in the USA, West Germany, France, Japan & the UK*, London: National Economic Development Office, p.13.

WHERE ARE WE TODAY?

Estimates about the number of managers in the UK vary significantly. This is mainly due to lack of a common definition of what a management role is (for example, is a first-line supervisor a 'manager'?) In 2002, the Council for Excellence in Management & Leadership (CEML) reported that there were between 2.5 million and 6 million managers in the UK but 'most likely' between 4 million or 4.5 million. CEML also found that SMEs represent over 52% of the UK's total turnover (excluding finance), they employ over 56% of the UK workforce and have over 1.75 million managers within them. CEML also reported that 36% of organisations believe their managers are not proficient. The same research also found that:

- 24% of managers are qualified to degree level, compared to 65% for the professions.
- 12% of the female population of working age are managers; 20% of men.

So why is leadership and management development so important? According to the Department for Trade & Industry:

'A key factor in the success of any company, especially one that is innovating and growing, is the quality of its management and leadership. Innovative ideas are often the vision of inspired leaders.'[76]

Through CEML and other initiatives, the present Government has invested significant funds into investigating what constitutes 'good' management, analysing the current state of management development in the UK and producing a strategy to ensure that the UK has the managers and leaders of the future to match the best in the world.

Another review, this time of skills in general in the UK, carried out by Lord Leitch, was published in 2006. The Leitch Review had a wider remit than CEML, as the team involved in compiling it assessed skill shortages in general rather than just focusing on leadership and management. The recommendations from the review have a strong

---

[76] DTI website, 2007 – now Department of Business, Enterprise & Regulatory Reform, http://www.berr.gov.uk.

focus on raising people's aspirations and awareness of the value of skills and on emphasising the link between productivity and performance and the need to be world class. There are obvious implications here both for the development of leaders and the ways in which leaders develop others. In both of these reports, there is little discussion of how workers (including managers) should experience development in a way that makes it meaningful and enduring for them. There is an assumption that, if it is 'demand-led', then it satisfies needs; but where does the need for real and transformative learning come in? How do managers know what their needs are, so that they can demand that they be fulfilled?

In this section, we propose a way in which learning to be a leader is at the heart of the leadership development process. By learning, we mean real and permanent changes in behaviour that have a significant impact on the individual *and* the organisation. Our model of leadership development promotes an evaluation-led approach, which ensures that there is a focus on the benefits that individuals and businesses can expect to gain from leadership development.

FIGURE 11.1: THE NLA MODEL OF LEADERSHIP DEVELOPMENT

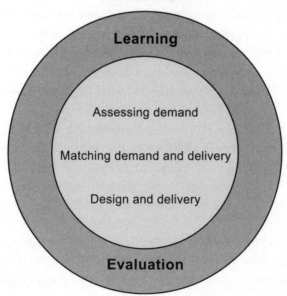

There are four elements to our model, which are discussed in this section of the book. We considered creating a model comprising boxes with lines linking them together but this created problems as the lines ran in every direction, making the diagram difficult to understand. We also considered creating a cyclical or circular model, like the systematic training cycle shown in **Figure 11.2**, but this did not help us to portray the inter-connectedness of activities, which are the essence of excellent leadership development practice.

FIGURE 11.2: THE SYSTEMATIC TRAINING CYCLE

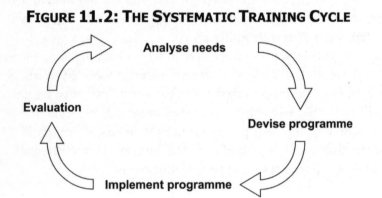

The difference between the NLA model of leadership development and some of the cyclical models is that we do not assume that one activity naturally follows another in a clearly-sequenced way. Such models do not present a clear view of reality but show how things might look in an ideal, systematised world. The NLA model illustrates the interdependencies between all of the elements.

In **Figure 11.1**, we have placed 'Assessing demand', 'Matching demand and supply' and 'Delivery' at the centre of the model, as these are the key activities that we go on to describe later in this section. 'Evaluation' and 'Learning' are shown surrounding these key activities; this is because we believe that it is important to bear them in mind constantly, whilst assessing development needs, commissioning and developing programmes and in delivering programmes.

Evaluation constitutes an activity in its own right and there is a chapter in this book devoted to it. However, evaluation should not be seen as a 'once and for all' activity; it should be built into each stage of the process. The same goes for learning; a heightened awareness of the principles of learning can help to ensure that leadership development programmes are focused on the needs of learners and the outcomes that might be achieved as a result of being involved in the programme rather than the actions of the trainer or the facilitator.

In summary, our philosophy of leadership development is evaluation-led and learner-centred. We now move onto explaining the ideas that underpin this philosophy and look at some of the practices which are associated with it.

'EVALUATION-LED' LEADERSHIP DEVELOPMENT

Leadership development providers are becoming increasingly aware of the need to design and deliver learning interventions that add value to a business or an organisation. The approach described here ensures that evaluation is considered throughout the process of commissioning, designing and delivering any learning programme. Training and development can no longer be an 'act of faith'; it must make a real difference to the individuals, groups and organisations that are committing time and resources to it. In this chapter, we explain the NLA model of evaluation and give examples of the tools and techniques that can be used to collect and analyse evaluation data.

Our model of evaluation-led leadership development characterises evaluation as an activity integrated into the whole process rather than something tagged on at the end of a project. This is often called 'formative' evaluation, as opposed to 'summative' evaluation. Formative evaluation is concerned with learning about the value of the intervention whilst it is happening, as a way of improving the experience of learners, and it may include a re-negotiation of the original learning objectives. In the NLA model of leadership development, evaluation is not a treatment applied to learners and the intervention but something that happens collaboratively and has beneficial outcomes for a range of stakeholders. According to Professor John Burgoyne at Henley Management College, the benefits of building evaluation into a programme are that it:

- Helps you justify investment in development in terms of organisation impact.

- Helps you improve the design of change initiatives and management development.

- Helps you revise and adapt what you are doing as it develops, rather than when it is too late.

- Helps organisations hang on to what they learn from initiatives, and maximise their ability to revise and fine-tune initiatives as they unfold.

Here, we offer three key questions that may assist leadership development providers to build in evaluation into their learning interventions and to place the learner at the centre of the process:

1. Are learning needs identified and articulated? Is there a recognised demand for this type of learning or does that demand need to be created or leveraged?

Most leadership development programmes do not just 'happen': there is normally some kind of identified need. These needs may include giving leaders a more strategic focus, in order to help the organisation reach its long-term objectives; helping them to acquire a particular set of skills; or re-defining and articulating organisational values in a period of rapid change. In large organisations, these programmes may be based on an in-depth, structured needs assessment of all managers, using a technique such as 360 degree appraisal and / or psychometric techniques. In smaller organisations, leaders rely on less sophisticated techniques and often must recognise and identify their own learning needs.

There are two main types of learning need:

- **Retrospective:** A retrospective need arises when a manager has a gap in the skill set required for his / her current job or role.

- **Prospective:** Prospective needs are based on looking at how the business might change and grow in the future and the knowledge, skills and attitudes needed to achieve this growth.

It is much easier to identify retrospective learning needs; they are normally picked up when it becomes obvious that a particular skill or piece of knowledge or experience is missing in an individual or group. Prospective needs require a much more thoughtful analysis of where the business and the individual are going. In many cases, the development of particular skills and knowledge may be the key to business growth and, for example, may enable the company to exploit a growing market. Boydell & Leary (1999) offer a useful framework (**Figure 11.3**) for needs identification, showing how needs can be identified in three areas – the individual, the group and the organisation – and at three levels – implementing, improving and innovating. Their matrix illustrates how retrospective and prospective needs are characterised throughout an organisation.

FIGURE 11.3: BOYDELL & LEARY'S MODEL OF NEEDS ANALYSIS

LEVEL OF BUSINESS BENEFIT	AREA OF NEED		
	Organisational	**Group**	**Individual**
L1: Implementing: doing things well	Meeting current organisational objectives	Working together to meet existing standards and targets	Being competent at the existing level of requirements
L2: Improving: doing things better	Setting higher objectives and reaching them	Continuous improvement teams	Having and using systematic continuous improvement skills and processes
L3: Innovating: doing new and better things	Changing objectives and strategies	Working around boundaries to create new relationships and new products / services	Being able to work differently and more creatively with a shared sense of purpose

In larger organisations, needs identification may occur through the use of competency frameworks,[77] which are normally integrated into a performance management system. The use of competencies clarifies organisational priorities in terms of learning and development and helps individuals to identify their own learning needs and careers.

---

[77] For examples of competency frameworks, go to http://www.highways.gov.uk/jobs/3341.aspx or http://jobs.healthcarecommission.org.uk/appform/Healthcare%20Commission%20-%20Competency%20Framework.pdf.

2. Is the learner at the centre of the process?

The most common error in planning leadership development interventions is deciding upon the solution before the problem has been properly diagnosed. We often get swept along with the idea of sending all our managers on a qualification course or buying in some coaching time and then we try to fit the needs analysis with pre-prescribed learning outcomes. If evaluation is to be built into the process, it is at this stage that we should ask crucial questions about the value of the intervention, both in terms of meeting the needs that have been identified and whether it is likely to create an appropriate learning space to meet individuals' needs. The focus should be clearly on the learner and their learning.

'Learning' is a term that is increasingly used in everyday language. Successive UK governments have emphasised the idea of 'lifelong learning' in an attempt to encourage members and potential members of the workforce to become involved in education and training. Similarly, the terminology used in schools now has much more of a focus on 'learning', as opposed to 'education'. The notion of learning, used in these contexts, embraces the idea of the learner becoming much more active in the process of gaining new knowledge or understanding rather than being a passive recipient. Whether this is actually the case in the examples cited is open to discussion.

A short and simple definition of learning is given by Bass & Vaughan:

> *'Learning is a relatively permanent change in behaviour that occurs as a result of practice or experience'.*[78]

Central to this definition is that learning:

- Persists.
- Is not due to some temporary (probably physical) condition.
- Only occurs when there is an observable change in behaviour.

Traditional, classroom-based education and training courses are based on the principle that, if learning has occurred, we should be able to see

---

[78]   Bass, B.M. & Vaughan, J.A. (1966). *Training in Industry: The Management of Learning,* Belmont, CA: Wadsworth, p.8.

and measure the effects of it. Furthermore, we can manipulate conditions and experiences to ensure that individuals and groups exhibit the desired 'terminal' behaviour.

This approach evidently ignores the role of individual and group cognitive processes and casts the learner as an unsuspecting and unthinking being, ready to be changed in whatever way is deemed desirable by the 'educator'.

As we have already outlined above, Malcolm Knowles[79] offers a humanist cognitive approach that aids our understanding of adult learning and the conditions required to stimulate learning. He talks about how adults differ from children in their approach to learning in respect to issues such as their needs to know; their self concept; their role and past experiences; their readiness to learn and the way adults are motivated to learn in order to perform the tasks they confront in their life situations.

This so-called 'andragogical' approach helps leadership development providers to design and deliver learning interventions in a way that is capable of motivating and inspiring learners. Some questions you might ask yourself before commissioning or designing an intervention are:

- Why is it important for our learners to develop their skills, knowledge or attitudes in this subject area? Will they know that it is important or do we have to contextualise it for them before inviting them to participate?

- Does the learning design reflect a certain amount of learner autonomy and does it give them scope to personalise and internalise the content of the learning?

- Will learners be given an opportunity to reflect on previous experiences and to examine them critically, in a way that 'brings forward' learning?

- Will learners be able to use the learning content immediately? How can you ensure that you contextualise the learning in such a way to create positive learning transfer?

---

[79] Knowles, M (1990). *The Adult Learner: A Neglected Species*, Houston: Gulf Publishing Co.

Experiential learning

The most popular model of learning, in the sense that it is used as the basis of programme design in a range of management learning contexts, is Kolb's (1984) Experiential Learning Theory.[80] Kolb's theory is based on the principle that learning is best conceived as a process, rather than as the attainment of a set of outcomes, and that this process leads to the creation of knowledge.

FIGURE 11.4: KOLB'S EXPERIENTIAL LEARNING CYCLE

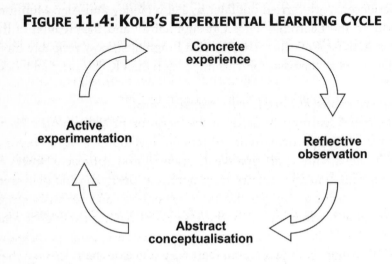

Learning is a four-stage cycle of concrete experience, observations and reflections, formation of abstract concepts and generalisations and testing implications of concepts in new situations. Kolb sees these four elements as distinct stages in the learning 'cycle': a continuous process through which we shape and re-form ideas and knowledge. Knowledge is not about outcomes that can be stored and retrieved as required, rather it is created by a continuous process of reflection on the experiences of our everyday life. In this view of learning, the processes of action to reflection to conceptualisation and then analysis happen in discrete steps and learners may have control over this learning process.

Kolb's theory has had a major impact on the way that management training and development (and to some extent, education) is devised and delivered. Kolb's learning cycle is one of the most well-known

---

[80]   Kolb, D.A. (1984). *Experiential Learning*, Englewood Cliffs, NJ: Prentice-Hall.

illustrations in management education and development, offering an insight into learning as a process rather than a set of outcomes, and his theory has changed the way in which many managers have experienced training and development, by emphasising the trainee rather than the trainer as the prime source of learning.

Kolb also first introduced the notion that individuals have their own personal learning styles that are shaped by their personality and experience. Work carried out later by Peter Honey and Alan Mumford produced the Learning Styles Questionnaire[81] and the creation of the terms Activist, Reflector, Theorist and Pragmatist, now probably more widely used as the basis for learning design than Kolb's original work.

When experiential learning becomes too experiential
Experiential learning is used as the basis of programme design in many contexts, particularly in leadership development. It has become synonymous with a participative, learner-centred approach. However, there is sometimes a tendency for programme designers and deliverers to over-concentrate on the learners' experience and to misinterpret experiential learning as solely the process of having experience after experience. This may result in fantastic feedback from participants who have enjoyed a programme but may not necessarily change their behaviour as a result.

If experiential learning is to result in meaningful changes in the way our learners lead their teams or organisations, then, as programme designers and deliverers, we need to be aware of 'meta-level' processes. Here, we are mainly concerned with giving learners the opportunity to reflect in a meaningful and productive way. Central to the NLA model of leadership development is the idea that learning should involve reflection that both leads to a change in behaviour and helps learners to examine the principles upon which they base their practice as a way of creating thoughtful and self-critical practitioners.

Reflection
It is tempting, particularly when using Kolb's model, to characterise reflection as something that happens independently; as if managers

---

[81] Honey, P. & Mumford, A. (1992). *The Manual of Learning Styles*, Maidenhead: Peter Honey Publications.

and leaders can somehow 'stand back' from a situation, weigh up the pros and cons and then make a balanced judgement. Of course, their work rarely happens in such an ordered and measured way; managers' jobs are frenetic and usually involve dealing with a number of issues and priorities at the same time. By the same token, managers rarely confront problems that have standard 'textbook' answers. In reality, practitioners are solving novel problems in unique circumstances and they need to experiment and rethink previous practice in order to solve them. So this internal reflection happens naturally for those in a leadership role and relies heavily on tacit, rather than explicit, knowledge. In other words, successful leaders and managers need the 'know-how' that comes with practice, experience and learning. This is not to say that knowledge in its traditional sense is not needed but that tacit and explicit knowledge should work in tandem to create and shape good leadership practice.

When reflection happens on a simple level, learners change their behaviour without changing the set of perceptions on which these actions are based. This may produce better results in the short-term. The NLA concept of learner-centredness in the context of leadership development entails individuals being able to question both their behaviour and the mental models it is based upon. Jack Mezirow calls this 'transformative learning'; Chris Argyris calls it 'double-loop' learning. When this happens, leaders and managers do not just change their behaviour on a one-off basis but begin to question the foundations of their practice. A firm emphasis on double-loop learning in leadership development interventions helps to create insightful and change-orientated leaders.

3. Is there a clear picture of what the outcomes of the learning intervention will be, in terms of learner behaviours and benefits to the individual and the organisation?

This question seems to repeat the issues discussed earlier under the heading of needs analysis. However, this stage is different, in that it emphasises the need to keep learning objectives in clear focus and to start evaluating them both in terms of whether they are being reached and whether they are still appropriate and useful. So this is a midstage evaluation; there is not necessarily a requirement for an *independent* evaluator at this stage, although this may help. The ability to carry out this type of evaluation by leadership development providers themselves is one of the hallmarks of good practice; if something is not working, there is no point in continuing for the sake or ease of it. Acknowledging that elements of a programme need to change is not an admission of defeat but a recognition that the learning needs of the organisation and its groups and individuals are dynamic in nature.

If the learning programme is one that takes place over a period of time, it is worth attempting to collect some interim measures of return on investment (see **Chapter 12**). It may be that learners are enjoying, and individually benefiting from, a programme but that the behavioural outcomes will have little or no impact on the business. The identification of critical success factors for projects, such as those used in action evaluation (again, see **Chapter 12**) may also be helpful.

In summary, evaluation-led leadership development exists when a culture of feedback is created in a learning programme or intervention. This feedback can be obtained from a number of sources: the learners themselves, providers and facilitators and other stakeholders on whom the programme is likely to have or designed to have, an impact. The NLA model is designed to emphasise the need for a high concern both for the learning experience itself and the likely impact of changed behaviours on the business. The remainder of this part of the book provides more suggestions on how to provide formative and future-focused learning interventions for leaders and potential leaders.

12

COLLECTING THE EVIDENCE THROUGH EVALUATION

T his chapter examines a number of approaches to evaluating leadership development activities. Central to effective evaluation is a clear sense of purpose – here, we set out a range of purposes for evaluation and offer approaches and activities that fit with each of these. We emphasis our belief, set out in **Chapter 11**, that learning and evaluation are linked inextricably and we make a case for learning-centred evaluation approaches being compatible with models of distributed leadership.

Leadership development interventions fall into two categories; here, we use the terms 'abstract' to signify course-based interventions that normally have fixed learning outcomes and 'person-centred' approaches for those with more personal development objectives. We propose that evaluation techniques take account of the nature of the learning intervention itself, rather than simply using off-the-shelf techniques, as a way of encouraging the type of reflection that is central to effective learning and behaviour change.

MOTHERHOOD, APPLE PIE & EVALUATION?

Evaluation of training and development is generally agreed to be a 'good thing' and something that we should all 'do', whether on a macro level to measure the impact of public or private spending or at the micro level of finding out how individuals have reacted to learning activities. We all agree that evaluation is something that should be done but there are no clear guidelines on the 'best' way to evaluate, given the range of circumstances in which evaluation takes place.

Evaluation is often a messy business, especially when we are trying to identify causal relationships between learning activities and job performance; how can we be sure that something that happened to a trainee on a course led to, for example, their increased confidence in leading their team? It becomes ever more difficult when a further link is attempted to organisation performance measures like profit, turnover or gross value added (GVA), yet this is what many evaluations set out, and often fail, to achieve. The reason they fail is that a whole range of factors impact on human behaviour, so trying to narrow it down in this way is an enormous over-simplification. Therefore, it is ironic that this kind of 'scientific' examination of a learning event, often carried out by an external evaluator, is usually seen as the ideal type of evaluation: an objective, desensitised, systematic appraisal of inputs and outputs.

The first step in any successful evaluation is to clarify its purpose; we use Mark Easterby-Smith's[82] framework of purposes to show how and why different approaches produce different results. We then make a distinction between two main types of learning activity in which we would expect readers of this book to be involved; we have called these 'abstract' and 'person-centred' learning and suggest ways in which evaluation approaches might differ in each case. The next section deals with some of these approaches to evaluation and examines how useful they might be in evaluating leadership development activities. We then go on to propose a view of evaluation which has learning as its central purpose, building on the ideas about evaluation-led leadership development put forward in **Chapter 11**. We also offer a number of

---

[82]   Easterby-Smith, M. (1994). *Evaluating Management Development, Training & Education,* Aldershot: Gower.

approaches to evaluation that seek both to measure and to monitor the effects of the event or activity and to encourage and stimulate learning as part of the evaluation process itself. Finally, there is an examination of the key problems associated with evaluation, especially the evaluation of leadership development, and some suggestions as to how these might be overcome.

WHY EVALUATE? WHAT CAN YOU EXPECT TO ACHIEVE?

We have not been entirely positive so far about the benefits of evaluation and it is true that the amount of work involved in collecting and analysing data often is not reflected in the outcomes. The first step any evaluator needs to take is to decide on the purpose or purposes of their work. Mark Easterby-Smith suggests four possibilities here:

Proving

If your evaluation sets out to prove the impact and worth of training and development, usually using some kind of cost-benefit analysis, then it falls into this category. This notion of 'proving' is linked to assessing the value of a programme. It is often used by public bodies to assess the payback from investments in projects and may include an analysis of gross value added, which measures the contribution to the economy of a particular sector or industry. Other approaches to measuring return on investment (ROI) are discussed later in this chapter.

A less formulaic approach to proving the value of training and development activities is the use of 'stakeholder evaluation',[83] which seeks the views of all those with an interest in the programme (for example, learners, trainers, bosses, funders) in order to assess its value. Stakeholder evaluation can be likened to the 360 degree appraisal used by some organisations, producing a rounded or balanced picture, in this case, of a learning programme rather than merely representing either the trainer's or learner's views, as is normally the case.

---

[83] An approach defined by Professor John Burgoyne, Henley Management College.

Improving

This approach is also known as formative evaluation and is focused on improving the learning programme. The type of information collected here is particularly useful to the trainer, as it deals with process rather than outcomes, and is useful in assessing which elements of the programme were particularly useful for learners. However, learners may often be impressed with elements of the programme that are particularly enjoyable rather than potentially impactful on their work performance. So this method of evaluation is not only partial, but may have little to do with the learning experience and more to do with the 'fun' factor in learning programmes. If we were to use this approach as our sole means of evaluation, trainers might be tempted to become crowd-pleasers rather than facilitators of learning.

Learning

When evaluation activities have learning as a central purpose, then they become collaborative, involving learners, trainers and evaluators (of course, very often, trainer and evaluator are the same person). In this approach, there is no dividing line between the measurement of process and outcomes because they are interlinked. There is no artificial divide between what the trainer does and how the learner reacts to it, followed by an 'objective' assessment of cause and effect. The 'learning' approach to evaluation recognises the fluid and unpredictable nature of many learning experiences and acknowledges the influence of learners on any programme, rather than suggesting that trainers have total control in manipulating processes and outcomes. If we think about trainers having a leadership role, then this 'learning' approach to evaluation fits well with the NLA's approach to distributed leadership.

Controlling

This approach to evaluation is most often seen in large-scale learning efforts aimed at producing consistent behaviours in a large group of people. It is characterised by standardised and closely-measured learning outcomes and is typified by the way in which the UK Government uses the National Curriculum to standardise learning outcomes and encourages parents to judge schools on the basis of their

National Curriculum test results. National Vocational Qualifications are used in a similar way and individual or collective attainments are used as measures of evaluation. Many organisations use their own competency frameworks as a way of both designing and evaluating learning programmes.[84]

In addition to the above purposes, we might add another – influence.[85] This is an acceptance that findings from evaluation can be used to persuade others – for example, the continuation of a programme might require convincing results.

You may find that an evaluation has more than one purpose, which is perfectly fine as long as they are not competing. The most common purposes of evaluating are proving and improving but decisions about which methods to use should be based on the needs of the programme and stakeholders.

DECIDING ON THE EVALUATION APPROACH

To illustrate how different approaches to evaluation are likely to be needed in a range of leadership development situations, we draw a distinction here between two types of learning activity. The first we have called 'abstract' learning approaches, covering learning programmes that generally take place off-the-job and have relatively fixed learning outcomes. The second category we have called 'person-centred' learning, which includes techniques such as coaching and mentoring.

Abstract learning approaches

Many leadership development interventions take the form of courses; these can be as short as half a day in duration or may involve attendance over a long period of time, particularly when they lead to a qualification. There will normally be a prescribed set of learning outcomes to be achieved by learners on the programme, and one of the first stages of evaluation is to attempt to measure whether these

---

[84]   For an example, go to http://www.highways.gov.uk/jobs/3341.aspx.

[85]   Influence as a purpose of evaluation is suggested by Mumford, A. & Gold, J. (2004). *Management Development Strategies for Action*, London: CIPD.

learning outcomes have been achieved. In practice, however, this is sometimes the first *and* final stage.

Donald Kirkpatrick's[86] 'chain reaction' model of evaluation is the approach that most trainers and developers attempt to employ. It is based on the principle that there are five distinct stages of learning and change, which can be measured to gauge the impact of the learning programme:

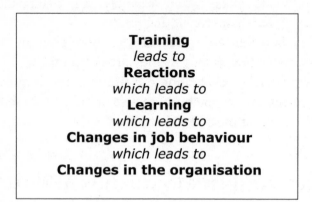

Training
leads to
Reactions
which leads to
Learning
which leads to
Changes in job behaviour
which leads to
Changes in the organisation

In this chain reaction model, evaluation starts with a formative look at the processes used on the programme, moving onto the measurement of reactions – how trainees felt about the programme and how they responded to various aspects of it. These reactions lead to learning, measured against learning outcomes set for the programme; in some cases, evaluators may also try to assess whether there are any unintended learning outcomes. This learning should result in individuals changing their behaviour in the workplace (in line with the learning outcomes), which ultimately will lead to changes in organisational performance.

If you asked a large group of trainers which approach to evaluation they used, many of them would say the Kirkpatrick or chain reaction model. In practice, the chain often breaks down when attempts are made to link learning outcomes achieved on the course to the effects on job behaviours, and evaluation then is limited to an assessment of

---

[86]   This model shown here is based on Kirkpatrick, D. (1959/60). 'Techniques for evaluating training programmes: Parts 1 to 4', *Journal of the American Society for Training & Development*.

reactions through an end-of-course questionnaire and some testing of learning outcomes that can be built into the programme methodology. The reason this happens is that it is very difficult to measure learning transfer – when learners attempt to apply what they have learnt in a training room in their normal work environment. One study shows that on average, 62% of employees apply what they learn in training on the job immediately after the training event, 44% are still applying it six months later and 34% one year after training. It's quite worrying to think that 38% of employees who attend training courses do not change their behaviour at all as a result of attending. Other studies suggest the transfer of learning over time seldom rises above 10%!

The final step in the chain reaction evaluation process is the most problematic of all. This is particularly the case with leadership development, because the way in which organisational impact can be measured is much less quantifiable than, for example, trying to assess the bottom-line effect of a compulsory accident-prevention programme in the workplace. The problem lies in trying to disentangle, and then re-connect, individual learning and organisational performance in a sterile cause-and-effect way rather than acknowledging that a wide range of factors impact on how organisations perform and trying to understand which of these can be affected by leadership development initiatives. It is for these reasons that many organisations do not try to evaluate leadership beyond the reactions stage and accept its contribution to organisation performance as an 'act of faith' – although we think they can do better.

Person-centred approaches

These approaches to leadership development, such as mentoring, coaching and action learning, are much more clearly-focused on personal development, which is not fixed to any specific learning outcomes. Although it is possible to apply a chain reaction approach to person-centred learning, it is unlikely to produce helpful results. Rather than 'proving' the value of the development initiative, evaluation in this case is much more likely to focus on 'learning' and can be a collaborative activity between trainer (or coach / mentor) and learner. This does not mean that quantitative techniques cannot be used; in fact, when the evaluation focuses on one person, it is easier to produce figures to show how their learning has had an impact on the business. Later in this chapter, we examine how certain evaluation techniques normally used in person-centred learning can be transferred successfully to abstract learning activities.

THE CONTEXT & LEVELS OF EVALUATION

So far, we have looked at the purposes of evaluation and made a distinction between the types of learning event to be evaluated. Work that we have carried out in the Northern Leadership Academy suggests that there are three levels of evaluation as shown in **Figure 12.1**.

FIGURE 12.1: LEVELS OF EVALUATION

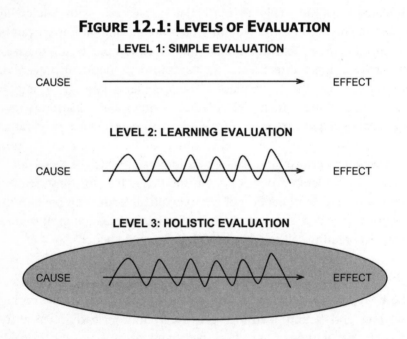

LEVEL 1: SIMPLE EVALUATION

CAUSE ⟶ EFFECT

LEVEL 2: LEARNING EVALUATION

CAUSE ⟶ EFFECT

LEVEL 3: HOLISTIC EVALUATION

CAUSE ⟶ EFFECT

Level 1: Simple Evaluation

Simple evaluation is typified by the chain reaction model; the evaluator identifies the prompts for change and then attempts to connect these to their effects. It is a simple and easily-understandable way of collecting and analysing evaluation data. Evaluators are likely to be detached from the process, and perhaps from the learners themselves, preferring to use 'hard' data to draw their conclusions. This data includes information from end-of-course questionnaires to assess the learners' reaction, job performance information and ROI (return on investment) calculations.

Level 2: Learning Evaluation

At this level, we are still interested in cause and effect, but there is a much heavier focus on the learning that happens in order to bring about those changes. Here, we are more interested in the process of learning than at Level 1 and, probably, this will involve including learners in the evaluation.

Level 3: Holistic Evaluation

Here, we acknowledge that cause, effect and learning are all important, but that any learning programme operates within a system and there is a need to understand how the system impacts on the learning event and *vice versa*. This involves asking some 'why?' questions about the design and delivery of the programme and some 'how?' questions about the impact on colleagues and on the bottom line. Evaluating at this level provides information that can be used to inform organisational policy and strategy.

EVALUATION TECHNIQUES

Having decided the purpose and level of your evaluation, the next step is to decide on the techniques best suited to them. Choice of evaluation techniques depends on two main issues:

- The level at which the evaluation is being carried out.
- The time that has elapsed since the learning event took place (of course, some evaluation happens *during* the event itself).

Figure 12.2 gives examples of techniques and the appropriate level and time-scale for their use.

FIGURE 12.2: EVALUATION TECHNIQUES

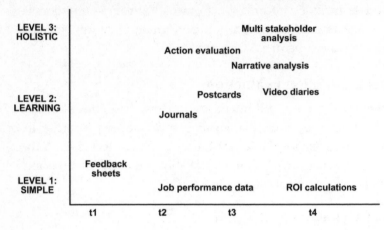

Level 1 evaluation techniques

Feedback sheets

End-of-course questionnaires, or 'happy sheets', are often what pass for evaluation on many programmes and, although they attempt to assess both the effects of the learning event and the learners' reactions to it, they provide little more than a glimpse of how learners intend to apply their learning and are rarely followed up. Such questionnaires have become part of the ritual of training and development activities; trainers feel that they should issue one and learners feel short-changed if they don't complete one. But what good do they really serve, apart from making the trainer feel good (or bad) about themselves, and for gaining feedback on things that can only be changed for the next group of learners (quality of the accommodation and food)? Evaluation should be concerned with assessing how learners learn and change rather than awarding marks for the trainer's performance. This type of evaluation also encourages learners to place all of the responsibility for their learning on the trainer, rather than acknowledging that this responsibility should be shared.

Next time you are involved in a leadership learning event, try omitting the questionnaire and use one of the methods at Level 2 instead.

ROI calculations
This is the holy grail of evaluation for many people; the ultimate in the 'scientific' approach. ROI is a technique derived from financial analysis that uses the formula:

$$\% \; ROI = \frac{Gain \; from \; investment}{Cost \; of \; investment} \times 100$$

On paper, this looks sensible and usable, in practice it is quite the opposite, particularly for leadership development activities. Calculating the costs of a programme are relatively easy, if somewhat time-consuming and disputable; the problem lies in defining gains made from a leadership development programme. For example, if the aims of a programme are to promote better communication and to encourage managers to become more entrepreneurial, then it becomes difficult to make clear links between these objectives and business outcomes, because of the effort and uncertainty involved in disentangling all of the variables involved, as well as the likely time-lag between learning and outcomes. If, however, you were to use one of the Level 2 or Level 3 techniques suggested below, you could still measure impact on the business without losing the thread of how learning, action and business performance are connected.

Level 2 evaluation techniques

As we saw in **Chapter 11**, our model of evaluation-led leadership development characterises evaluation as an activity integrated into the whole process rather than something tagged on at the end of a project. Evaluation is not a treatment applied to learners and the intervention, but something that happens collaboratively and has beneficial outcomes for a range of stakeholders.

Level 2 evaluation techniques blend learning and evaluation by making evaluation part of the individual's learning process. Three techniques are described here; these are examples of level 2 evaluation that are particularly suitable for leadership development rather than an exhaustive list.

Journals

It is a widely accepted fact that reflection is one of the key components of effective learning. Nearly all of us reflect on what happens to us on a daily basis, perhaps mulling over the day's events on our journey home from work, thinking 'out loud' to our family and friends or coming up with bright ideas in the shower. Most of the time, these reflections are strikingly consistent or those bright ideas never come to fruition. The reason for this is that the link between reflection and action is often tenuous, because our thoughts are often fleeting, or because we are distracted, or because it's easier to put off doing something about them.

Learning journals are designed to help learners turn reflection into action. Leadership development programmes should give learners ideas about and insights into their own practice as a leader, but the learning and the evaluation of that learning should not stop there. Recording these thoughts and making decisions helps learners to think about how they might change their behaviour as a result and prompts them to take action.

If your leadership development programme is workshop-based, encourage learners to think about and write about what happened and what they learnt from it. Specific questions might include:

- How does this learning relate to the goals that you have set yourself?
- How will you change your practice as a result of it?
- How are you changing as a leader and a learner?

Excerpts from a learning journal used on one of our NLA programmes are given in the box below:

Section 1: Where am I now?
The first step in creating a journal is to think about where you are now. What kind of leader are you? What do you find easy about your role? What are the most challenging aspects? Which parts do you enjoy and which are the bits you dread? What are the key leadership challenges that you currently face?

Section 2: Where do I want to get to?
What are your learning goals? Why are you willing to devote so much of your time to this programme? What do you want to get out of it? This may seem like a simple question to which the answer may be 'I want to be a better leader' but what does that mean for you? Try to be specific in the goals that you set.

Section 3: How have I learnt best in the past? How will this help me now?
Everyone learns in different ways. Some people are happy to listen and 'soak up' other people's knowledge, whereas others can't sit still and listen for more than 20 minutes. Some learners can find inspiration in a book, but others don't get past the first two pages. Some will tell you that there is no substitute for experience, whereas others feel nervous at the thought of the 'error' in trial-and-error learning. What kind of learning works best for you? How will you use this consciousness of your learning skills to help you now? Who do you need to help you?

Although a learning journal should be personal to the learner who has written it, their contents provide an excellent source of evaluation material. One technique that we have used at the NLA is to ask learners to provide a 'highlight report' of the programme, using their journal as the basis. In this way, we collected information about three things:

- **The process:** Learners' highlight reports gave us evidence about which elements of the programme had the most impact upon them and, from 35 individual 'learner stories', we were able to assess which topics had the most resonance for learners and which learning methods they responded most positively to. This is a useful way of measuring the impact of a programme on learners, without setting up a scoring system for the trainers or the accommodation.

- **Learning transfer:** By asking learners to record how they had changed their practice as a result of the programme, we gained some excellent examples of learning transfer. We also found out which parts of it had little effect on learners' behaviour.

- **The extent of 'learning to learn' skills:** Leadership development interventions should aim to give learners new skills and insights, in terms of their ability to learn in a range of circumstances. Evidence from journals showed us how our programme had impacted on this essential by-product of leadership learning interventions.

Postcards

Leaders are busy people who cannot always find the time to complete detailed evaluation reports. Evaluation-led leadership development does not start and end with the 'input' of a programme or the interchange of a coaching session; evaluation should reinforce and extend the learning.

'Postcards' provide a useful way of getting feedback on a learning event, at the same time as encouraging learners to reflect on how their behaviour may have changed and to maintain their consciousness of their learning objectives and goals. You can ask learners to reply to an e-postcard – an email or series of emails asking open-ended questions, requiring short answers – or you can use the old-fashioned way of supplying them with a series of real postcards with questions printed on them. The questions you ask will depend on the objectives of your programme but here are some examples that might help:

What was the most significant part of the learning programme for you? Why?

How have you changed your leadership practice as a result of something that happened to you on the programme?

When do you find time to reflect on your leadership practice?

What have you learnt today?

What have you told your colleagues about the programme?

How will you use your learning from the programme to benefit others in your organisation?

Both journals and postcards involve leaders writing about their experiences; the written word is a powerful way of encouraging learners to give a considered view of how an experience may have helped them to improve their leadership practice. However, you may wish to use the spoken word to collect evaluation data and the next technique provides an example of how to do this.

Narrative analysis

'Narrative' is a broad term covering stories, myths, fables, tragedy and painting.[87] When we use this phrase, we mean that we are interested in the stories that leaders tell of their learning experiences. Giving learners the opportunity to tell a story out loud helps us to capture the unique nature of individual experience and provides a richness that the written word does not always produce. As part of the learning experience, recounting events and feelings to someone else helps leaders to make sense retrospectively of what has happened to them and often provides new insights in the telling of the story.

Storytelling can happen collectively as part of an evaluation 'event' that brings learners back together to reflect on how a programme has affected their leadership practice or stories can be collected from individuals. Try using a digital voice recorder to capture what is said rather than trying to write down snippets of information; you can even encourage individual learners to record their own accounts of learning and practice and to send them to you for evaluation purposes.

Level 3 evaluation techniques

Evaluation at this level takes account of the causes and effects of the changes brought about by the programme, the learning that prompts these changes and the impact, not only on individual learners, but on a range of stakeholders within the system in which the programme is operating. This system might be confined to an organisation, including its customers and suppliers, or it may be much wider than one organisation, especially if the programme is publicly-funded.

Two Level 3 approaches are described here: action evaluation places an emphasis on goal-setting by stakeholders, whereas multi-stakeholder evaluation involves a retrospective analysis of the effects of a programme.

---

[87] For a comprehensive account of the nature and significance of organisational stories, see Gabriel, Y. (2000). *Storytelling in Organisations,* Oxford: Oxford University Press.

Both of these Level 3 approaches require the evaluator to collect and analyse 'hard' (countable and quantifiable) and 'soft' (concerned with perception, attitudes and feelings) data. They allow him / her to achieve a well-rounded picture of how an event or programme has touched anyone with an interest in it. At first sight, these approaches can appear daunting in terms of the number of people to be consulted and the array of accounts and opinions to be listened to. However, they are scaleable; you can choose to collect information from a sample of people who represent your stakeholder groups and you do not necessarily have to interview them all face-to-face.

Action evaluation

Action evaluation (AE) first was developed as a technique aimed at conflict resolution within organisations. Stakeholders of a learning event or programme are identified and are asked to set goals and to discuss the values and motivations associated with those goals. Actions, based upon the achievement of these goals, are then agreed. The goals become the focal point of the learning and the action taken, and provide a touchstone for learners' reflection and feedback. Goals are continuously reassessed and redefined in the light of action taken and insights gained. The dynamic nature of goals means that evaluation is integrated into the programme and becomes the focal point of learning.

Multi-stakeholder evaluation

As the name suggests, this approach to evaluation is designed to ensure that anyone who has an interest in, or is likely to be affected by, a learning event is asked for their assessment of its value. Multi-stakeholder evaluation is a thorough and balanced picture of how a programme has impacted on learners, sponsors, funders, colleagues, managers, customers and the wider community. It should be designed to measure both its intended and unintended effects so, although data can be collected about whether the programme has achieved its objectives, evaluators are also interested in stakeholders' experiences and perceptions of it.

TIPS FOR MEANINGFUL & USEFUL EVALUATION

It is easy to feel overwhelmed by the choice of approaches to evaluation or to decide that it is too complicated and time-consuming to bother with at all. We hope this chapter has persuaded you that there is a point to evaluating leadership development activities and that it can be integrated into the learning itself.

Some of the key points we have covered here are:

- Measure learning and behaviour change in learners' *not* the trainer's performance.

- Goal-setting and reflection are key elements of learning and evaluation.

- Start with the end in mind (as Stephen Covey might say) – think about evaluation before the programme commences.

- Remember that evaluation can occur at different points in time and at a range of levels.

- Look for 'hard' and 'soft' data and think about why you need it and how you might use it – what is the purpose of your evaluation activity?

- Consider how evaluation activities can help to transfer learning from the training to the work situation.

- Consider as many stakeholders as possible when evaluating a learning programme.

13

COLLABORATING
PARTNERSHIPS

T o further the NLA's vision of a new paradigm
of 'leaderful' communities, we offer a blueprint
for a way forward as to how this might be
achieved. The chapter outlines how evidence gained
from the considered activities of the think-tank can be
put into action in sustainable and practical ways.

We believe that the key steps outlined have the
potential to move the region forwards.

Our vision of leadership development is one of
collaboration, where responsibility for development is
distributed to those close to communities where the
relationships exist and the expertise is available.

CREATING A DISTRIBUTED MODEL OF LEADERSHIP

The Northern Leadership Academy began with a vision of the need to maintain a rich and diverse, enterprising, pro-active community of leaders that could sustain itself and grow. By so doing, this community quickly would become a social and entrepreneurial magnet that would draw into the region other talented individuals who would prosper and, in turn, reinvest in the region. We promoted an image of 'leaderful' communities, underpinned theoretically by a distributed view of leadership where leaders can come from all walks of life, from all levels in organisations. We believed that a shift in mindsets in this direction could feed a spiral of improving productivity and growth.

We also have a view that there were many different ways in which the development of leaders could take place and that, although there are clear differences between sectors, there would be principles of good practice that would apply to each sector, around which development activities could be designed.

Two years on, we realise that we still have a path to travel and, although the vision is still clear and the landscape is recognised and known, the exact route to our goal still needs some careful consideration. What we have done though is made some plans for the journey and begun to take the first steps.

BASING DEVELOPMENTS ON EVIDENCE

We have set in process an ongoing method of collecting and considering evidence relating to the practice of leadership, management and enterprise development. Starting from a position where we believed we already knew a great deal, we soon realised that we knew rather less. We wanted to become 'thought-leaders,' whereby we could present convincing ideas that could transform thinking and practice throughout the North.[88] However, in order to do this, we need to maintain the ability to collect evidence of what was working and

---

[88] For more on thought-leadership, see McCrimmon, M. (2005). 'Thought-leadership: A radical departure from traditional leadership', *Management Decision* 43(7):1064-70.

what was not. As we have shown in **Chapters 10** and **11**, evidence of quality is not easy to come by and evaluation, even at a basic level, is often reduced to simple reactions. Nevertheless, we began with a mentality of openness to the evidence; a learning process for all that could not be limited, as shown in **Figure 13.1**. At the outset of the project, we took the view that we did not have all the answers and that we needed to get close to those who were working in the different fields and gain the benefit of their knowledge and experience, whilst at the same time not neglecting the research that is constantly being undertaken, as well as the evaluations of activity on the ground.

FIGURE 13.1: A LEARNING PROCESS FOR THOUGHT-LEADERSHIP

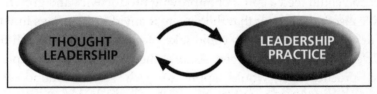

We sought evidence of all kinds, such as systematic reviews of literature, evaluation reports of programmes completed, stories told by advocates of particular approaches and emerging features, workshops with managers and practitioners and so on. It still remains the case that we cannot point to anything definitive that shows a linear cause-and-effect of one approach against another or a truthful statement about what works. For example, in a systematic review of evidence for effective leadership in the contexts of the public and voluntary sectors and in SMEs, we found sparse evidence.[89]

A similar result was found in other reviews:

'... the sheer volume of studies to date had not in themselves helped to clarify the picture. Vast numbers of empirical studies were inconsequential in outcome and often trivial in design. The 'theories' of

---

[89] See the review by John Lawler, Richard Thorpe and Jeff Gold, available from http://www.northernleadershipacademy.co.uk/portal/server.pt/gateway/PTARGS_0_343_1 99413_0_0_18/.

leadership were lacking in breadth and were often addressing different phenomena.'[90]

However, while there certainly was a lack of clarification and definition, we could begin to point to some features of the emerging picture, so long as we recognised that a final statement was some way off.

DESIGNING GOOD PRACTICE GUIDELINES BASED ON EVIDENCE

The emerging evidence on leadership, management and enterprise development, however incomplete, could be re-presented as suggestions and guidance for those who seek to commission, design and assess activities. These are the Design Principles presented in **Chapters 5, 8** and **9**.

FIGURE 13.2: A MODEL OF HOW THOUGHT-LEADERSHIP CAN LEAD TO PRINCIPLES OF GOOD PRACTICE FOR PROGRAMME DESIGN

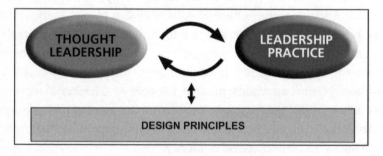

The importance of the Design Principles is that they are a statement of our best attempt to understand the evidence. They certainly are not complete and need constant testing in the various contexts of practice. However, we recognise the need for more and better evidence. For example, publicly-funded leadership programmes for SMEs need to

---

[90]   Storey, J. & Mangham, I. (2004). 'Bringing the strands together', in Storey, J. (ed.). *Leadership in Organisations: Current Issues & Key Trends,* London: Routledge, p.339.

adopt a far more rigorous approach to measurement over longer time periods. Crucially, we need evaluation that moves from Level 1 to Levels 2 and 3, as outlined in **Chapter 11**. It is worth saying that we still find examples of significant projects that hardly assess impact, even at Level 1.[91]

We already have begun to turn the principles into a more practical tool for different contexts. As 'thought-leadership', seeking to spread the influence of our work, we need to find favour with others who make decisions about resources, while responding to their needs. For example, the first SME design principle is concerned with engagement with identity and interests. The evidence still is emerging here, but we do know that, for most managers in SMEs, learning becomes possible when it is related to their concerns, problems and desires. So, this prompts some key questions that can help consider activities for SME managers, such as:

- Is there a process to engage hard to reach managers?
- How are concerns, problems and desires identified?
- Is the situation and the history of that situation explored?
- How is the manager's story accessed?
- Is the next stage of that story in evidence?
- Is there an opportunity for managers to explain their personal interest?

The Case Example we presented at the end of **Chapter 7** seemed to show how such questions can provide for a firm basis for engagement. We know already that such guidance has helped those involved in SME leadership development.

---

[91] We write at a time when the Department for Innovation, Universities & Skills has announced a three-year programme of leadership development for SMEs, which tripled the budget, although there is little evidence of impact beyond immediate satisfaction from previous programmes.

DEVELOPING A STRUCTURE FOR CONTINUOUS IMPROVEMENT

'Thought-leaders' need to be champions of the principles they espouse. They need to close the gap between words and action. This meant that our small deliverables projects needed to be based on principles of what worked, but also provide a means of collecting more evidence through evaluation, as shown in **Figure 13.3**.

FIGURE 13.3: HOW EXPERIENCE IN THE FIELD CAN FEEDBACK INTO A VIRTUOUS CIRCLE OF LEARNING THAT ENSURES DESIGN PRINCIPLES ARE CONTINUOUSLY IMPROVED

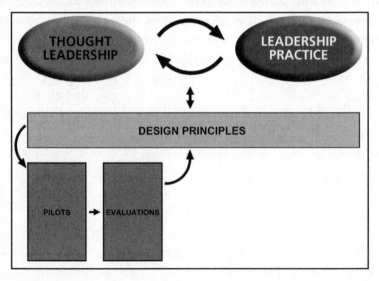

The NLA has funded 26 pilot projects, each of which reflected some aspect of what the evidence suggested was good practice or what was lacking in leadership, management and enterprise development. For example, we know very little about the needs of the voluntary sector, so engagement occurred in a variety of forms – workshops, forums, conversations. All have been evaluated to provide evidence for the Design Principles. Among the SMEs, we know that one-to-one mentoring or coaching is the preferred option for learning by many managers. We wanted to know how this occurred and whether value was added, which could eventually result in both benefit for the business but also a preparation by managers to pay for their help. We do have some indicators that this is occurring. We also have evidence of the power of action learning and growth programmes, if that is the preference of managers.

ENGAGING & REACHING OUT TO STAKEHOLDERS: A DISTRIBUTED APPROACH

'Thought-leadership' that promotes new ideas needs others to respond to those ideas. However, we recognise that there are many stakeholders and each will have their own interests to advance. As a consequence, we realised at an early stage that it would be important to engage with them, whenever possible face-to-face, in order to find where there might be mutual advantage in working together. This is distributed leadership in action, finding where the power and the influence lies and attempting to act in such a way that creates action for the benefit of the region as a whole. We recognise that these stakeholders would not change their own ideas easily, and so there needs to be an ongoing process of dialogue to allow different voices to be heard, assumptions surfaced and modified and challenged. For this to happen, mutual recognition is vital. We were very concerned that the NLA did not appear as an all-knowing 'Big Brother'. We knew we knew a great deal, but recognised there was a lot we did not know and needed to learn! Our approach, therefore, was to invite others as collaborating partners as shown in **Figure 13.4**.

We saw that the future of the NLA, and the development and enactment of principles, lay in a form of working that allowed different partners with different histories and interests and skills to work together. As a consequence of their own experience, many had been adhering to the principles of good practice provision for a considerable period of time. Most professional providers (but not all) undertake their own research and evaluations and, of course, learn from experience and adjust their practice as a natural part of their activity.

FIGURE 13.4: HOW PROVIDERS CAN BE CONNECTED TO THE DELIVERY & EVALUATION-LED DEVELOPMENT PROCESS

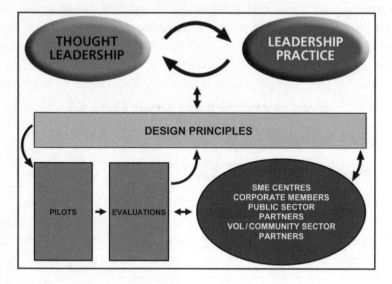

We also recognised that collaborative working would require a great deal of trust, which could not be taken for granted, and that the facility to argue together, so that we could leverage knowledge to enable the spread of what worked throughout the North, whilst at the same time sharing and capturing our learning, would not be easy. So, we need to provide opportunities to generate and create knowledge through action and to capture it through evaluation as evidence. If we advocate ideas, such as the importance of strategic space for managers and leaders, we needed to help create these, both within and between partners. In such spaces, knowledge can be shared, assumptions surfaced and challenged, tensions explored and new possibilities agreed. One appealing image is that of tying different strands of expertise together like that of a strong 'knot' – what has been called 'knotworking'.[92]

We have made most progress with the creation of, first, 10 and, then, 17 SME centres throughout the North. To varying degrees, each

---

92   Engeström, Y. (2004). 'New forms of learning in co-configuration work', paper to the Department of Information Systems' *ICTs in the Contemporary World* seminar, London School of Economics, January.

centre already had a record of SME leadership development. Most had contributed to our understanding in developing principles. We acknowledge that the first 10 were all existing universities; we saw these as proving the most fertile ground for collaboration. Our offer was to join with us to further our understanding of what works in leadership, management and enterprise development and to work with the SME design principles. In return, we wanted to work with each centre to spread the idea of collaboration, both within the institutions but also outwards toward local partners, as shown in **Figure 13.5**.

FIGURE 13.5: THE STAKEHOLDERS WITH WHOM THE CENTRES MIGHT USEFULLY ENGAGE

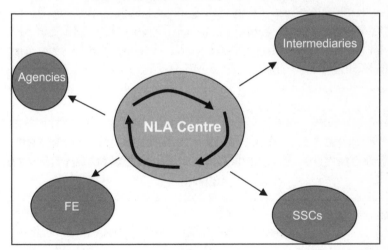

We highlight two elements here. First, a strategic learning process around leadership, management and enterprise development at the heart of the centre itself. This means a critical examination of approaches and offers but also finding out about expertise within each institution. For example, most universities are fragmented, with little effort to explore beyond traditional boundaries. But leadership and enterprise are cross-faculty issues. Where there is any semblance of connection with life outside the university, there will be a connection with an interest in leadership and enterprise development. We also have evidence that, when a cross-faculty approach is taken, the mutual benefits of sharing knowledge and progressing ideas can soon become clear to all; it is well worth the effort.

Second, each centre can look to form links with key groups and individuals outside the university or college. We highlight providers as key players, including Chambers of Commerce, that are successful in working and earning their living from helping SMEs. Many have great experience and can pass this on to managers, if the correct links are made. There is mutual learning for both university and providers from collaboration, just as much as for the FE colleges and work-based learning providers. Sector Skills Councils have a crucial role in stimulating demand for leadership development, following the 2006 Leitch Review. However, we know they also need help in completing this activity and it remains to be seen whether they have the resources to do so. Finally, there are the key agencies such as Business Link, the RDAs and the LSC. They often are sources of funding by competitive tender and, with the crucial drive towards business support simplification, a co-ordinated offering by centres in partnership with others, working with the design principles explained in earlier chapters, can pay dividends.

FIGURE 13.6: A NETWORK OF NETWORKS – HOW THE EVALUATION-LED DEVELOPMENT PROCESS MIGHT LINK TO CENTRES

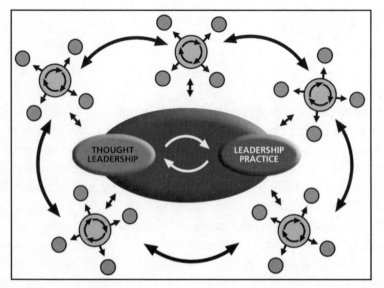

Looking ahead, we can see the growth of the ideas of centres as hubs of a network which in turn combine to provide a network of networks as shown in **Figure 13.6**.

We are beginning to see the idea of a network infrastructure in the North gaining support. The idea is that centres develop internal capacity, by seeing themselves as the hub of a local network. Each then can connect with other networks, as appropriate – for example, for regional or sub-regional projects. Most importantly, whatever is done is evaluated and provides evidence to the thought-leadership process. In return, each network gains the benefit of collective learning that can be disseminated among their partners.

We know this image looks strong on paper and principles. We also know that it still will require dialogue, persuasion and argument to make it happen. However, we feel this is just the kind of leadership the North has been waiting for.

BIBLIOGRAPHY

Adair, J. (1983). *Effective Leadership*, London: Gower.

Alimo-Metcalfe, B. & Alban-Metcalfe, J. (2005). 'Leadership: Time for a new direction?', *Leadership* 1(1): 51-71.

Argyris, C. (2004). *Reasons & Rationalisations: The Limits to Organisational Knowledge*, Oxford: Oxford University Press.

Bass, B.M. & Vaughan, J.A. (1966). *Training in Industry: The Management of Learning*, Belmont, CA: Wadsworth.

Bell, L., Bolam, R. & Cubillo, L. (2002). *A Systematic Review of the Impact of School Leadership & Management on Student / Pupil Outcomes*, Research Evidence in Education Library 1, London: EPPI-Centre, Social Science Research Unit, Institute of Education.

Bennett, N., Wise, C., Woods, P. & Harvey, J.A. (2003). *Distributed Leadership: A Review of Literature,* Nottingham: National College for School Leadership.

Bennis, W. & Nanus, B. (1985). *Leaders*, New York: Harper & Row.

Blake, R.R. & Mouton, J.S. (1964). *The Managerial Grid*, Houston: Gulf Publishing.

Burns, T. & Stalker, G.M. (1961). *The Management of Innovation*, London: Tavistock.

CEML (2002). *Joining Entrepreneurs in their World*, London: Council for Excellence in Management & Leadership.

Child, J. (1969). *British Management Thought: A Critical Analysis*, London: Goe, Allen & Unwin.

Clarkson, G.P. (2008). *Developing Leadership Research, Papers from the Northern Leadership Academy Fellows Conference 2007*, Leeds: Leeds University Press.

Cohen, W.M. & Levinthal, D.A. (1990). 'Absorptive capacity: A new perspective on learning and innovation', *Administrative Science Quarterly* 35(1): 128-52.

Collinson, D. (2005). 'Dialectics of leadership', *Human Relations*, 58(11): 1419-42.

Collinson, M. & Collinson, D. (2005b). *'Blended Leadership': Employee Perspectives on Effective Leadership in the UK FE Sector,* Working paper series, Lancaster: Centre for Excellence in Leadership.

Confederation of British Industry (2003). *Informality Works: A New Approach to Training for SMEs,* London: Confederation of British Industry.

Davies, H. (1980). *A Walk around the Lakes,* Feltham: Hamlyn Publishing.

Day, D.D. (2001). 'Leadership development: A review in context', *Leadership Quarterly,* 11(4): 581-613.

DfES – see Department for Education & Science.

Department for Education & Science (2003). *21st Century Skills: Realising Our Potential,* Norwich: HMSO.

Department for Education & Science (2005). *Skills: Getting on in Business,* Norwich: HMSO.

Drath, W. (2001). *The Deep Blue Sea: Rethinking the Source of Leadership,* San Francisco: Jossey-Bass.

Easterby-Smith, M. (1994). *Evaluating Management Development, Training & Education,* Aldershot: Gower.

Engeström, Y. (2004). 'New forms of learning in co-configuration work', paper to the Department of Information Systems' *ICTs in the Contemporary World* seminar, London School of Economics, January.

Farmer, R.N. & Richman, B.M. (1964). 'A model for research in comparative management', *Californian Management Review* 7: 57.

Finegold, D. & Soskice, D. (1988). 'The failure of training in Britain: analysis and prescription', *Oxford Review of Economic Policy* 4(3): 21-53.

Gabriel, Y. (2000). *Storytelling in Organisations,* Oxford: Oxford University Press.

Garengo, P., Biazzo, S. & Bititci, U.S. (2005). 'Performance measurement systems in SMEs: A review for a research agenda', *International Journal of Management Reviews* 7(1): 25-47.

Gold, J., Thorpe, R., Riley, M., Mayall, K. & Wadworth, B. (2007). *"Training, It's a Load of B*****ks": The Story of the Hairdresser & His Suit,* HRD Annual Conference, Oxford Brookes University, Oxford.

Grint, K. (2000). *The Arts of Leadership:* Oxford: Oxford University Press.

Gronn, P. (2000). 'Distributed properties: A new architecture for leadership', *Educational Management & Administration* 28(3): 317-338.

Handy, C. (1987). *The Making of Managers: Report on the Management Education, Training & Development in the USA, West Germany, France, Japan & the UK,* London: National Economic Development Office.

Heenan, D.A. & Bennis, W. (1999). *Co-leaders: The Power of Great Partnerships,* New York: Wiley.

Hersey, P. & Blanchard, K. (1988). *Management of Organisational Behavior,* Englewood Cliffs, NJ: Prentice-Hall.

HM Treasury (2003). *Enterprise Britain: A Modern Approach to Meeting the Enterprise Challenge*, Norwich: HMSO.

Holman, D. Pavlieka, K. & Thorpe, R. (1996). 'Re-thinking Kolb's theory of experiential learning: The contribution of social construction and activity theory', *Management Learning* 25(4): 489-504.

Honey, P. & Mumford, A. (1992). *The Manual of Learning Styles*, Maidenhead: Peter Honey Publications.

Jones, O., Macpherson, A., Thorpe, R. & Ghecham A. (2007). 'The evolution of business knowledge in SMEs: Conceptualising strategic space', *Journal of Strategic Change* 16(6): 281-294.

Kirkpatrick, D. (1959/60). 'Techniques for evaluating training programmes: Parts 1 to 4', *Journal of the American Society for Training & Development*.

Knowles, M. (1990). *The Adult Learner: A Neglected Species*, Houston: Gulf Publishing Co.

Kolb, D.A. (1984). *Experiential Learning*, Englewood Cliffs, NJ: Prentice-Hall.

Lambert, R. (2003). *Lambert Review of Business-University Collaboration: Final Report*, London: HM Treasury.

Lancaster Leadership Centre (2005). *Engaging Communities in Leadership: The Voice of the Future* conference, September, Lancaster: Lancaster Leadership Centre.

Lave, J. & Wenger, E. (1991). *Situated Learning: Legitimate Peripheral Participation*, Cambridge: Cambridge University Press.

Leitch, S. (2006). *Prosperity for All in the Global Economy – World Class Skills*, Final report of the Leitch Review of Skills, London: HMSO / HM Treasury.

McCrimmon, M. (2005). 'Thought-leadership: A radical departure from traditional leadership', *Management Decision* 43(7):1064-70.

Mumford, A. & Gold, J. (2004). *Management Development Strategies for Action*, London: CIPD.

Nicholson, N. (1997). 'Evolutionary psychology: Towards a new view of human nature and organisational society', *Human Relations*, 50:1053-78.

Nicholson, N. (1998). 'Seven deadly syndromes of management and organisation: The view from evolutionary psychology', *Managerial & Decision Economics* 19: 411-426.

Nicholson, N. (2000). *Managing the Human Animal*, London: Texere Books.

Nicholson, N. (2005). 'Objections to evolutionary psychology: Reflections, implications and the leadership exemplar', *Human Relations*, 58(3): 393-409.

Pedler, M. & Burgoyne, J.G. (2006). 'Distributed leadership', *View - NHSIII Journal* (11): 20-21.

Performance & Innovation Unit (2000). *Strengthening Leadership in the Public Sector*, London: Cabinet Office.

Perren, L. & Burgoyne, J.G. (2002). *The Management & Leadership Nexus: Dynamic Sharing of Practice & Principle,* London: Council for Excellence in Management & Leadership.

Perren, L., Davis, M., Kroessin, R. & Hannon, P. (2001). *Mapping of Management & Leadership Development Provisions for SMEs,* London: Council for Excellence in Management & Leadership.

Rae, D. (2004). 'Entrepreneurial learning: A practical model from the creative industries', *Education & Training* 46(8/9): 492-500.

Revans, R.W. (1998). *The ABC of Action Learning,* London: Lemos & Crane.

Rodgers, H., Frearson, M., Gold, J. & Holden, R. (2003). *International Comparator Contexts: The Leading Learning Project,* London: Learning & Skills Research Centre.

Ross, L., Rix, M. & Gold, J. (2005). 'Learning distributed leadership: Part 1', *Industrial & Commercial Training* 37(3): 130-137.

Senge, P. (1999). 'The gurus speak (panel discussion): Complexity and organisations', *Emergence* 1(1): 73-91.

Simon, H.A. (1957). *Administrative Behavior* (2nd ed.), New York: Macmillan.

Simpson, M., Tuck, N. & Bellamy, S. (2004). 'Small business success factors: The role of education and training', *Education & Training* 46(8/9): 481-491.

Spillane, J. (2006). *Distributed Leadership,* San Francisco: Wiley.

Stacey, R.D. (1992). *Managing Chaos: Dynamic Business Strategies in an Unpredictable World,* London: Kogan Page.

Stacey, R.D. (2003). *Strategic Management & Organisation Dynamics: The Challenge of Complexity,* London: Prentice-Hall.

Stogdill, R.M. (1974). *Handbook of Leadership,* New York: The Free Press.

Storey, J. & Mangham, I. (2004). 'Bringing the strands together', in Storey, J. (ed.). *Leadership in Organisations: Current Issues & Key Trends,* London: Routledge.

Thorpe, R., Holt, R., Macpherson, A. & Pittaway, L. (2007). *Studying the Evolution of Knowledge within Small & Medium-sized Firms,* London: Economic & Social Research Council / Engineering & Physical Sciences Research Council.

Thorpe, R., Jones, O., Macpherson, A & Holt, R. (2008). 'The evolution of business knowledge in SMEs', Scarbrough, H. (ed.). *The Evolution of Business Knowledge,* Oxford: Oxford University Press.

INDEX